CW00542515

SECRET
BIRMINGHAM

Tony A. J. Hewitt

AMBERLEY

Dedicated to Madeline Mills, a daughter of Acocks Green – once part of the Yardely district of Worcestershire – who served to defend her home, 1919–99.

Acknowledgements

Paul Smith for all the IT/typing.
Alan Godfrey Maps, Consett Co., Durham.
Birmingham and Midland Institute, No. 9 Margaret Street, B3 3BS.
Birmingham City Council Publications.
Cycling and walking map, Birmingham City Council Transport Department, No. 1 Lancaster Circus, Birmingham, B47DQ, 2015. PO Box 14439.
Public Art, Birmingham City Council, 1993.
Trail Map/Big Read, 2016.
Mathew Boulton – City Centre Walk, City Museum and Arts Trust.
Lunar Society – City Centre Walk, Birmingham Museums.
Birmingham Greenways, Heron Maps, PO Box 3008, Reading, RG1 9BU.
Birmingham Arboretum/Botanical Gardens Educational Charity.
British Waterways/Geo Projects – Birmingham Canal Navigations Map £4.75 – Geoprojects, No. 8 Southern Court, South Street, Reading, RG14QS.

First published 2017

Amberley Publishing
The Hill, Stroud, Gloucestershire, GL5 4EP
www.amberley-books.com

Copyright © Tony A. J. Hewitt, 2017

The right of Tony A. J. Hewitt to be identified as the Author of this work has been asserted in accordance with the Copyrights, Designs and Patents Act 1988.

ISBN 978 1 4456 6276 3 (print)
ISBN 978 1 4456 6277 0 (ebook)

All rights reserved. No part of this book may be reprinted or reproduced or utilised in any form or by any electronic, mechanical or other means, now known or hereafter invented, including photocopying and recording, or in any information storage or retrieval system, without the permission in writing from the Publishers.

British Library Cataloguing in Publication Data.
A catalogue record for this book is available from the British Library.

Origination by Amberley Publishing.
Printed in Great Britain.

Introduction

For a city the size of Birmingham it is impossible to only single out just ninety sites unique to it and its place in the Midlands. The city is 18 miles from Watford Gap on the present-day border with Staffordshire to the Lickey Hills in the south-west, and 11 miles across from Quinton, formerly in Worcestershire, to Sheldon Heath in the east, adjacent to Birmingham International Airport and Station, and the NEC.

It initially struck me to approach this book alphabetically to give every part of the city a mention – an 'Aston to Yardley' tour – but then some features cross several neighbourhoods, not least the aqueducts from Elan, canals from the Black Country, rivers of Bourne, Cole, Rea and Tame, and railways and their stations, which all made this city great in their own way.

As a historian the overwhelming urge was to approach this chronologically from at least the Romans at Metchley by the Worcester to Derby road, Rykneild Street. Here, a fort similar in size to Pennocrucium on Watling Street to the north was established.

The heart of 'Brum', as locals affectionately call their city, was established on the high ground occupied by St Martins (in the Bull Ring), by no means the oldest church in the city – that honour goes to St Edburghas in Yardley (c. 972).

In 1832 Nechells, Bordesley Green and Edgbaston formed a new borough of 183,000 people, which was granted in 1838. It became a county borough in 1888 and a city a year later with a population of over half a million. It had poached Harborne from Staffordshire in 1891, and Saltey Urban District Council and Little Bromwich Urban District Council and Balsall Heath all from Worcestershire.

Eleven years after the founding of the University of Birmingham, the four large surrounding districts, after Aston Manor borough in 1903 and Quinton in 1909, were Handsworth, Eardington, Yardley and Northfield with Kings Norton by 1911. Smethwick, a borough in Staffordshire, wasn't tempted to join the quartet – so that all 'Midland Red' buses were registered to Smethwick, Staffordshire.

Some things in plain sight have their secrets – apart from my uncle, who survived the sinking of the *Lancastria* when returning home from the BEF Army in June 1940 – one of the lucky out of 8,000! He later worked for the GPO telephones based in Ludgate Hill. Of all the 'Post Office' towers, the only square one is here, allbeit with chamfered corners to reduce wind resistance I'm told.

Today the city of Birmingham is Britain's largest local authority. It gained Royal Sutton Coldfield in 1974 under a nationwide local government reorganisation, making it Europe's biggest local authority. Birmingham has had a diocese for sixty-nine years. St Phillip's 'Wrenesque' Cathedral still survives but much of the core of buildings of the early city have been replaced – not surprising for a city that has 'Forward' as its motto.

Birmingham hasoften been quoted as a city of a 1,000 metal-bashing trades. It is only just shaking off its nickname of 'motor city', rightly or wrongly. In the 1960s and '70s it seemed to be dominated by the automobiles!

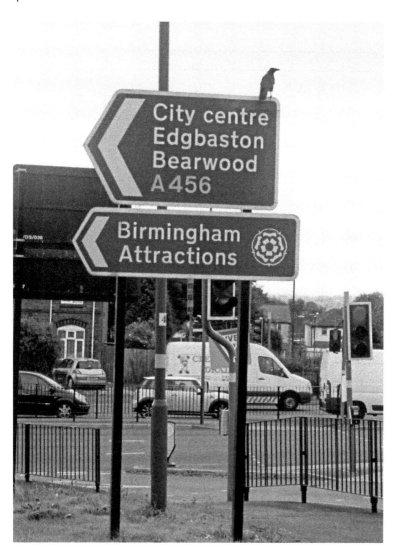

Yes, Birmingham has attracted at least 14 million visitors per year!

Mr Austin, who set up his huge car works at Longbridge, first drove a Wolseley. The Wolseleys hail from Staffordshire, illustrating that a successful city is one that can offer something to its surrounding region and attract skills from a broader base.

Foresight was a quality that the Cadburys, Chamberlains, Calthorpes, Marsons and other city fathers of the nineteenth century had. They endowed Birmingham with long-term investments: hospitals, schools, clean running water, its first university, and other cultural assets – not least the Town Hall. Its seen world premieres of great composers and acoustically it is only bettered by Britain's finest symphony hall – so good that Tangerine Dream held its concert there and not at the NEC. (Not to be confused by the NIA or NSC.)

But the basis of all this is down to BMW – Boulton, Murdoch and Watt – who are celebrated in Centenary Square for all to see. We shall see what remains to be found of their Birmingham and their contemporaries, upon which this city of Mercia is founded.

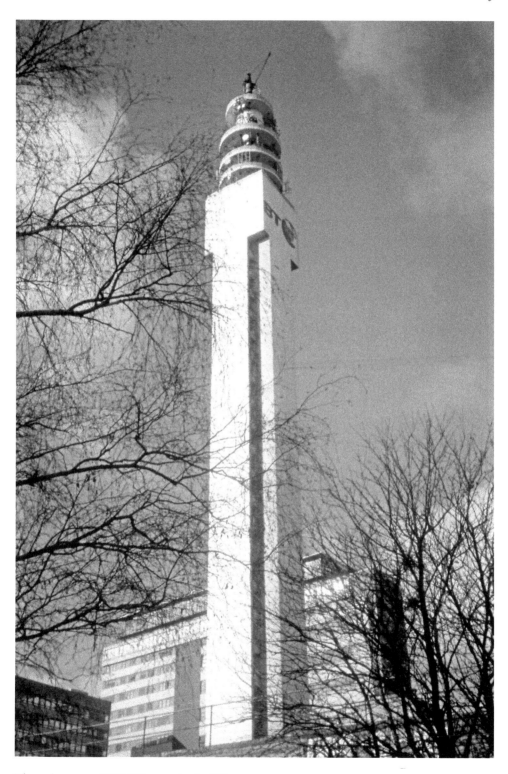

The only square GPO/BT tower in the UK.

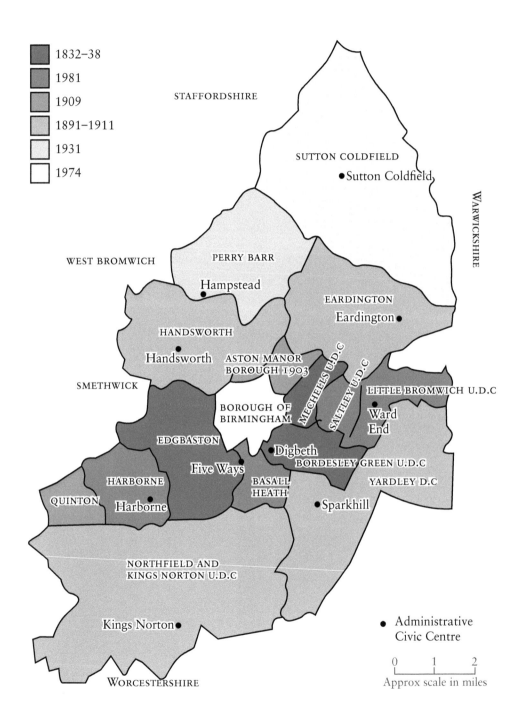

1832–38
1981
1909
1891–1911
1931
1974

STAFFORDSHIRE

SUTTON COLDFIELD
●Sutton Coldfield

WARWICKSHIRE

WEST BROMWICH

PERRY BARR
Hampstead
●

EARDINGTON
Eardington●

HANDSWORTH
Handsworth●

ASTON MANOR
BOROUGH 1903

MECHELLS U.D.C

SALTLEY U.D.C

LITTLE BROMWICH U.D.C

SMETHWICK

BOROUGH OF
BIRMINGHAM

Ward
End●

EDGBASTON

Digbeth●

BORDESLEY GREEN U.D.C

Five Ways●

HARBORNE

BASALL
HEATH

YARDLEY D.C

QUINTON

Harborne●

●Sparkhill

NORTHFIELD AND
KINGS NORTON U.D.C

Kings Norton●

● Administrative
Civic Centre

WORCESTERSHIRE

0   1   2

Approx scale in miles

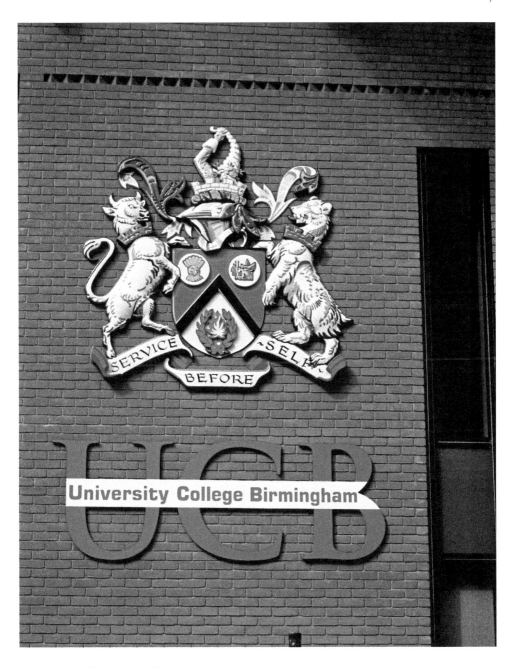

University College Birmingham.

Roman Metchley: A Fort on Rykneild Street by Bournebrook

Looking from Harbourne Bridge (once crossing the Lapal Canal) across the Woodgate/Bournebrook Valley, the modern fortress against disease stands in place of the Roman fort, once the crossroads from Roman towns at Pennocrucium, Letocetum, Alcester and Saline (Droitwich). The original Queen Elizabeth Hospital, opened early in her reign, has now been rebuilt for the twenty-first century. It is adjacent to the University of Birmingham on land given by Lord Calthorpe in the nineteenth century. It isn't the city's only major hospital but has been the centre of medical research since the mid-twentieth century. Its predecessor is now 'Centro House', which was established in 1779 in Newtown, just off St Chads Queensway.

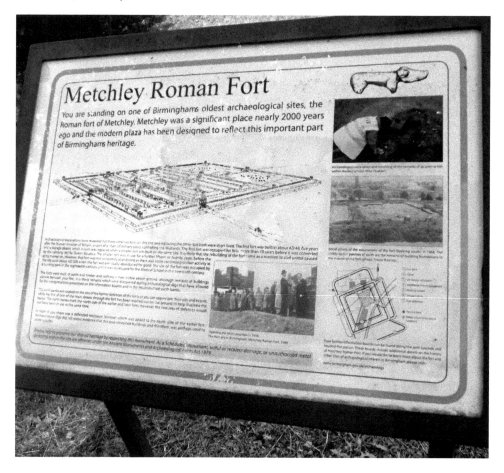

Metchley Roman Fort. (Courtesy of Elliot Brown under Creative Commons 2.0)

Weoley Castle – Birmingham's Only Castle

On the southern side of the Woodgate/Bourbrook Valley is sited a modest moated manor (of the type not unlike Stokesay Castle). Originally the land was granted to William Fitz Ansculf, later Baron Dudley. In 1264 Roger de Somery had acquired the land and had 're-crenelated', rebuilding the castle in stone. Inherited by the Berkleys, they lost it in 1485 after supporting Richard III at Bosworth. Confiscated by Henry VII, it was purchased by the Jervoise family, who rented out the land until 1809. Finally in 1929 the estate became a housing estate when the City Council purchased it.

DID YOU KNOW?

The Lapal Tunnel was an engineering nightmare due to constant subsidence, not least as it crossed the unconformity between two geological eras and rock types. The western boundary fault line created the upward movement of Silurian limestone of the Sedgely to Northfield ridge.

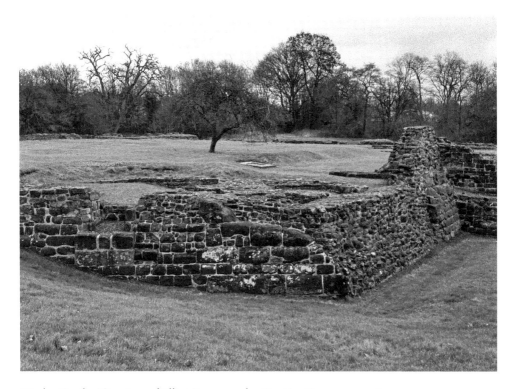

Weoley Castle. (Courtesy of Elliot Brown under Creative Commons 2.0)

River Rea – Waseley Hills and Longbridge

The photo below shows Birmingham seen from the source of its key river. The River Rea (pronounced 'Ray') has disappeared in many places in the city centre. It provided water power for many mills, originally for corn grinding; these were adapted for forging in the late seventeenth and early eighteenth century. The smithies gave rise to Birmingham's artisan metalworking until coal arrived as 'the fuel for growth'.

The Rea receives several smaller fast-flowing tributaries, such as the River Bourne, Wood Brook, Bourne Brook and Chad Brook, before it disappears in Highgate and Digbeth. It can be seen momentarily by Mr Bird's custard factory off Floodgate Street – now there's a clue – together with South Rea Street and River Street too.

Both the Rea and the Cole rise off the main British watershed to the south-west of the city centre and flow approximately the same distance to join the River Tame and eventually the Trent; they both contribute to the Trent's largest tributary. When they flood, they increase in size over fivefold, as can be evidenced in the city centre where the river bed is laid with blue brick to curtail erosion and damage to buildings. Underneath the Bordesley Viaduct the channel is over 20 feet deep.

DID YOU KNOW?

In ancient British language 'Cole' has the same meaning as 'Rea' in Anglo-Saxon, so Birmingham has two rivers with the same name.

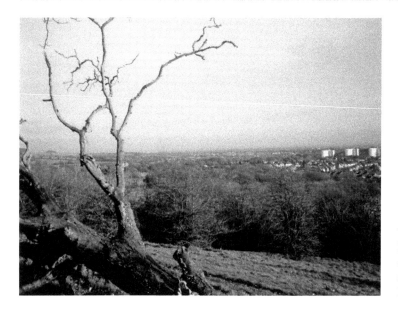

View from Waseley Hills, south-west of the city, the source of the River Rea.

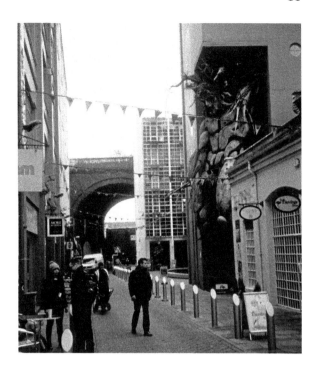

Rhubarb Yard, Deritend.

Underneath the Bordesley Viaduct

Mr Bird's custard factory is now an arts village behind the massive railway viaduct built to carry the GWR via Snow Hill Station to Wolverhampton, which were the most northerly termini of Brunel's Broad Gauge.

Birmingham's initial southerly expansion was along the Stratford Road (A34), which was paralleled by the Stratford/Grand Union Canal. The Warwick Bar isn't a new trendy tavern off the Bull Ring, but is in east Birmingham opposite the well-known Worcester Bar in the Gas Street basin. Here all the incoming goods off the Birmingham & Fazeley Canal, Coventry Canal, Stratford Canal and Grand Union Canal came together.

DID YOU KNOW?

The Bordesley Viaduct hasn't got all of its arches. It was designed to connect the London Stratford Railway to the Stour Valley Railway, allowing traffic to reach both Curzon Station on the London–Birmingham Railway and New Street on the London North Western Railway. The half that was built was used as a convenient siding to serve Moor Street Station and GWR's main station at Snow Hill.

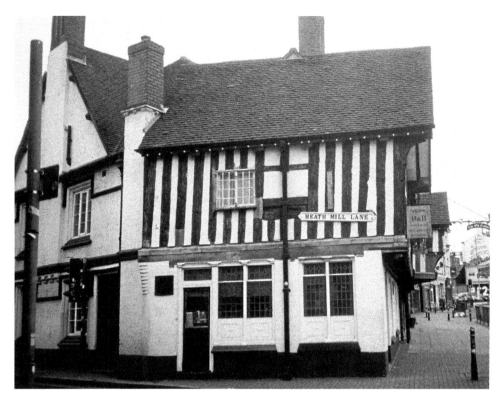

The oldest surviving pub in the city – The Crown.

Deritend and Digbeth

Digbeth has one of Birmingham's oldest buildings – the Old Crown Inn (*c.* 1368) at Deritend (now the east side of the dual carriageway), a few hundred yards from the custard factory at the junction of Heath Mill Lane and High Street. From here the view of St Martins in the Bull Ring illustrates the higher ground occupied by the city centre, especially with the new beehive behind St Martin's spire – but more on this later.

A ghostly presence lurks above Fazeley Street upon which the canal company offices, wharf houses and basin are found. Gone is the OXO wharf and HP Sauce factory, and the massive Curzon Viaduct is only half there. This was envisaged to link the Stratford line to the Midland Railway and indirectly to the LNWR line to London, but before we enter the Curzon Triangle we detour onto the canal towpath, once crossing the former canal office by Fellows, Morton and Clayton's new 1935 warehouse to reach the Warwick Bar. The Birmingham & Fazeley Canal, completed in 1790, was largely built up the Rea Valley from the Tame at Gravelley Hill – famous for a later mode of transport by another name: Spaghetti Junction.

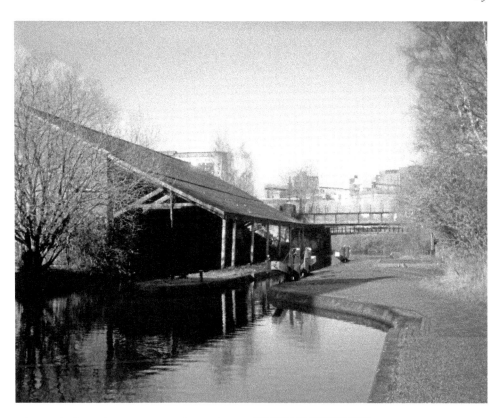

Above: The lesser-known 'Warwick Bar' by the Proof House.

Right: Fellows Morton and Clayton Canal Carriers 'New' warehouse.

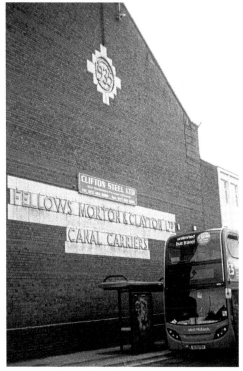

Canal City

The Grand Union Canal was the last canal to link into the network. It ran from Warwick and greatly widened in the twentieth century, which probably accounts for Fellows, Morton and Claytons 'new' warehouse of 1935. Sadly after the Second World War freight traffic steadily declined, so much so that by 1960 90 per cent of the waterways were threatened with closure!

Not originally a Birmingham Canal Co. 'cut', the Fazeley Canal, which linked to the Coventry Canal, went through such laboured gestation that in order to get the last link completed, the Birmingham Canal Network (BCN) bought the company out and built the missing section from Fradeley to Fazeley, thus bringing traffic off the Trent and Mersey nearer to the east coast ports. Previously the boats could wind their way via Walsall, offload there or wend their way to Ocker Hill Junction in Wednesbury and traverse the oldest link canal, built to bring coal from that town into Birmingham by James Brindley in 1769 – he has been commemorated in the new 'Brindley Place'.

With the Typhoo Tea basin behind, look for the 96 mile post – Grand Union miles from London – and go under the flying bridge to the right. Just beyond before Great Barr Street is the Rea Aqueduct behind Fellows, Morton and Clayton Ltd.

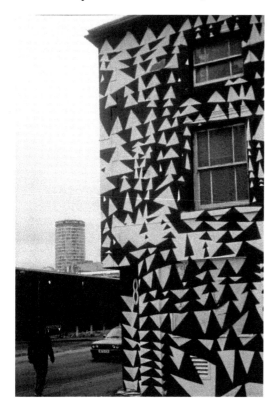

Rotunda seen from Curzon Triangle/ Haze House.

Curzon Triangle

Beyond the bridge is the Birmingham Proof House, established in 1813. To the right is Proof House Junction, through which all trains from Euston pass through to New Street Station via a tunnel under Moor Street and High Street. For waterway users the way to the Worcester Bar is also right and through the five Ashted locks and tunnel to reach Ashton Junction. We don't escape the Curzon Triangle so easily. Retrace back to Fazeley Street, named after the small Staffordshire mill town near Tamworth, famous for Sir Robert Peel's constituency home – Drayton Bassett Park – now the home of Britain's most famous locomotive, *Thomas* (but I digress; trains do this though –they take you to places you didn't intend!). There's one in Millennium Point, an LMS engine more powerful than Mallard. I'm getting ahead of myself, dazzled by the corner of Andover Street!

DID YOU KNOW?

James Brindley, a Cheshire lad apprenticed to a Leek millwright, made BMW's job easier by putting his canal right next to the famous Soho works, which is in Smethwick, Staffordshire, not Handsworth, also Staffordshire, pre-1911.

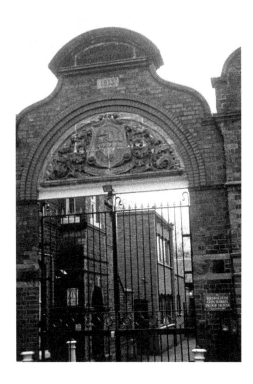

The Proof House gateway.

Now who's doubting the 'Curzon Triangle'? I've not seen anything this stunning in the Jewellery Quarter or the Village or by Lozells Ikon! Even the iconic Rotunda Tower looks trite against this razzle dazzle. Adjacent Banbury Street leads to the still functioning Gun Proof House, sited between the Euston Line and Warwick Bar canal junction.

Proof House

The imposing gateway of Proof House – there's only one destination on a horse down Banbury Street! At the top of the road is New Canal Street, which is aside Eastside Park. This expanse created by severing Queensway ring road is now the centre of regeneration, begun with the Millennium Point Think Tank Science Museum that replaced the city's previous museum in Newhall Street. It overlooks the former Curzon Street Station, Britain's first long-distance intercity terminal of 1838. All but the gigantic booking hall was demolished to make way for a rail freight terminal during electrification in the 1960s.

DID YOU KNOW?

BSA stood for Birmingham Small Arms Co. Ltd, later to become famous for their motorbikes.

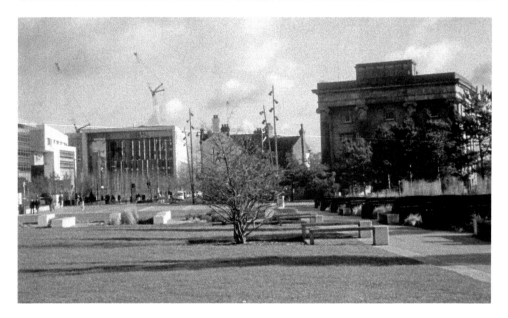

The new East Side.

Millennium Point

Curzon Street Station awaits the arrival of the twenty-first-century London Express on the HS2 line. Opposite is the Think Tank Science Museum, which houses the LMS Stanier Pacific *City of Birmingham* locomotive. At nearby Tyseley sister LMS Stanier engine *Princess Elizabeth* and LNWR Bloomer *Prince George* are part of a preservation revival in locomotive engineering – including some of the components for the LMS Patriot *Unknown Warrior*'s new build engine 45551. The well-known *Shakespeare Express* often pulled by GWR Hall or Manor class engines begins from the Tyseley depot.

Beneath our feet on New Canal/Meriden Street clean water is flowing in the trunk mains from the Elan Valley of Radnorshire.

By 2018, 180 years will have passed by since its construction – thirty years after the plaque was affixed to the classical portico of Curzon Street Station. Will it be receiving passengers by 2028? If this high-speed rail is all it's cracked up to be, then it's obvious where the third runway should be – Elmdon Airport (better known as BIA)!

Over the tracks in Saltley in the former Birmingham Railway Carriage and Wagon Co. works, founded by Joseph Wright in 1845, was the site of the Metro-Cammell works, builders of many London Tube train sets. Built to last, many are still giving service on the Central and Circle lines or the Isle of Wight! Here, too, the Virgin West Coast main-line tilting trains were assembled in the 1990s. Pity we had to import the Pendolinos from Italy, but Mrs Thatcher didn't understand the 'stick ability' needed when inventing cutting-edge technology. They could have been made up the line in Derby fifteen years before – the APT.

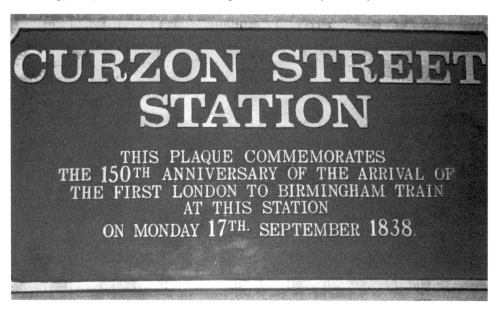

Curzon Street Station plaque – are we due a new addition?.

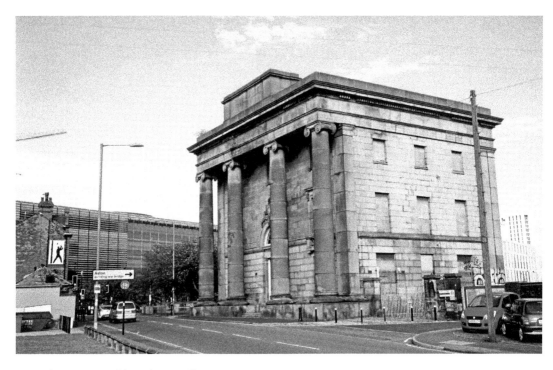

The 150-year-old Booking Hall, Curzon Street Station.

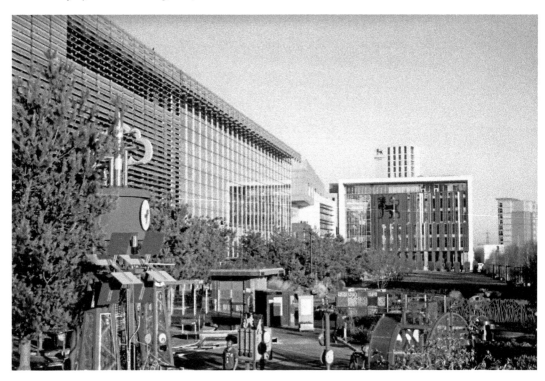

Think Tank/Museum of Science and Industry.

Think Tank Millennium Point

Think Tank is Birmingham's science museum; it was built in the 1990s as the Centre of Millennium Point, the focal point of the east end regeneration including Metropolitan College. Opposite is this neoclassical building. Curzon Street Station was the first termini of the London–Birmingham railway. It is difficult to believe this is just the Booking Hall and mimicked the London terminal at Euston.

The London–Birmingham Railway was the world's first long-distance intercity railway for passengers and the first station was called Vauxhall, now Duddeston, which opened in 1837. By 1846 the London & North Western Railway had been created and the New Street/ Grand Central was always intended to be the hub of Birmingham's railways. However, GWR built their line to Snow Hill in 1852, rendering the linking Digbeth–Duddeson viaduct superfluous – it still stands today, half complete!

Built over the former LNWR Curzon goods station and the Midland Brewery. Only Fox Street and Cardigan Street remain from the previous area. Millennium Think Tank is Birmingham's museum of science and technology. It incorporates the School of Acting and Dance. The area is mixed use development of businesses and higher education.

The City of Birmingham University has recently centralised many faculties in the £150-million new campus.

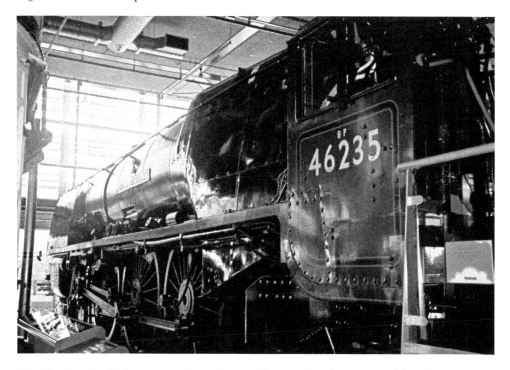

LMS Duchess Pacific locomotive *City of Birmingham* is the only survivor of this class.

It is anticipated that the new engineering technology college of the HS2 railway will be located on the east side near Aston University and City University.

On the parallel road behind is another new build – Mathew Boulton faculty of Birmingham Metropolitan College on Jennens Road.

Of all the twenty-one cities that gave their name to Stanier's LMS Duchess Pacific class of locomotives, only one, *City of Birmingham*, wasn't scrapped. The others were named after cities on LMS tracks, such as Lichfield, Coventry and Stoke-on-Trent – it had the longest name plate at 7 feet 6 inches. Built in Crewe, some were streamlined in 1933 and 'Coronation' Scot achieved the World Speed Record at over 114 mph on the Trent Valley/WCML at Whitmore Bank, near Madeley, Staffordshire. They were used on a long-haul routes, Euston to Glasgow and Liverpool; even though it could carry 10 tons of coal and 4,000 gallons of water, the engines were fitted with water scoops to enable non-stop running. The LMS locomotives hold the record non-stop on the challenging London–Glasgow route. These Pacific's had the greatest draw bar capacity of all British steam locomotives.

Bull Ring Market and the Aqueduct

The Bull Ring market is still open air. Since 1166 Birmingham has had a market charter, granted after Peter de Birmingham sponsored it. Rotten Park was the lord of the manor's

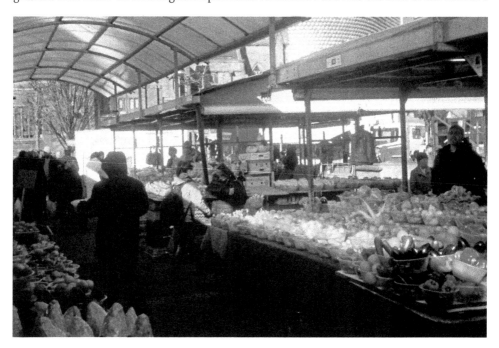

Birmingham still has an open-air market, which was first granted in 1166.

hunting estate. He later endowed St Thomas's Priory and hospital in 1286, now lost to us, but a frieze tableau can be seen in Old Square/Priory Queensway. How many Brummies realise that along Sherlock Street at the bottom of the market flows millions of gallons of water in the Elan Aqueduct – 75 miles long, being gravity fed on a 1:2,300 gradient and built in 1893 at a cost to the Corporation of £6 million. When completed in 1906, it was opened by Edward VII and Queen Alexandra.

Birmingham's mother church is St Martins in the Bull Ring. Here the de Birmyngham's vaults are to be found. The recently redesigned plaza affords views southward to Camp Hill, Cannon Hill and Bordesley. The resited Nelson Monument, once nearer New Street, was the cities tribute to Admiral Nelson and was erected in 1809 – the first in Britain.

DID YOU KNOW?

Birmingham has two cathedrals. In addition to St Martins, it has St Phillip's on Colmore Row and St Chad's – the patron saint of Mercia. It also has a Buddhist temple, central synagogue and central mosque.

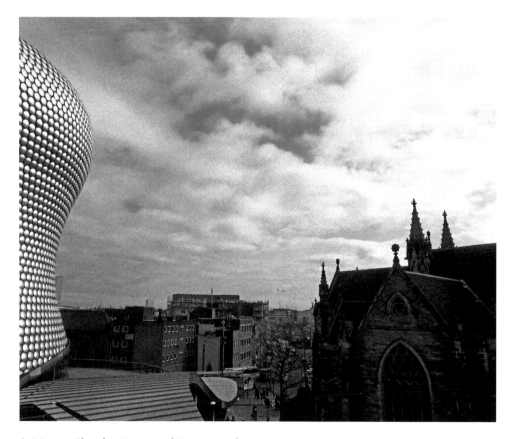

St Martins Church. (Courtesy of Dun.can under Creative Commons 2.0)

It surprises many people that Birmingham has firm links to the sea and the Royal Navy. The present day HMS *Daring* – a guided missile destroyer – has the freedom of the city. As big as a First World War dreadnought battleship, it is the class leader of eight vessels built on the Clyde. During the Second World War, a City class cruiser carried the name of Birmingham. It was built in 1936, serving in Home, Far East, Mediterranean and South Atlantic fleets until 1960. It was a sister ship of HMS *Belfast*. HMS *Forward* is the permanent RNR base, overseeing six training ships. Edgbaston's 32-million-gallon reservoir, built to supply the Birmingham Canal Navigations, is home to TS *Vernon*.

Adjacent to the canal reservoir is the Upper Edgbaston Waterworks, fed by the Frankley Reservoir of the Elan Aqueduct. This was originally linked by the Engine House arm at Soho in Handsworth.

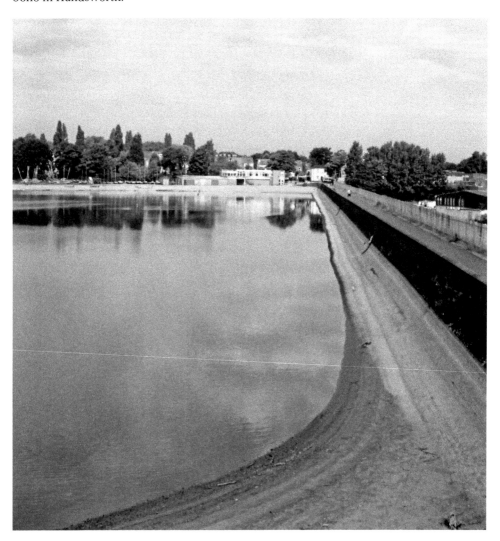

Edgbaston Reservoir.

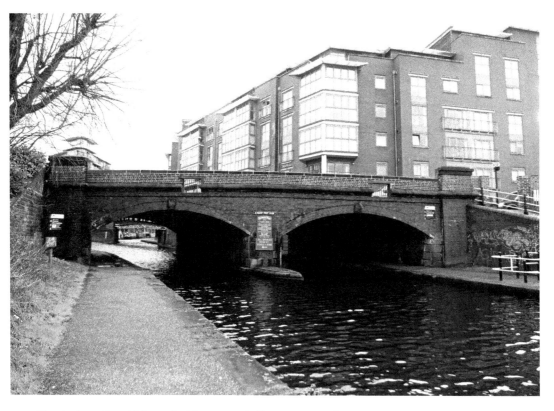

Birmingham Canal Network. (Courtesy of Elliot Brown under Creative Commons 2.0)

DID YOU KNOW?

Birmingham may have more canals than Venice but most of the mileage of the Birmingham Canal Navigations Co. waterways are in the Black Country of Staffordshire – but that's another story.

Nelson's Monument

The city's newest store is Nelson's backdrop – 200 years separate them. These railings appear to be the originals, not removed during the Second World War. Below this upper plaza are two memorials to recent conflicts. At an average of 320 feet above sea level, it is Britain's largest non-coastal city and well above the rise in sea level during this century. It will be a long time before the Navy can sail up the Tame into Brum.

St Martins in the Bull Ring

Birmingham was a regular target for the Luftwaffe during the Second World War. The height of the Blitz in Birmingham was during 1942. My mother joined the WAAF and served in RAF Signals until 1948 – maybe the bombing had something to do with that. In St Martins marketplace is a recently sculptured memorial to those Brummies killed in the Blitz.

After London and Merseyside, Birmingham received more tonnage of high explosives between 1940 and 1943 than any other. Over 2,200 citizens were killed and 3,000 seriously injured. Much of the new pre-war housing stock of 40,000 homes was damaged beyond repair. Neville Chamberlain, former city mayor and later prime minister, would have despaired, as he had officiated at the handing over of the 40,000th home in 1933 – had he not died in 1940. As local MP he stood against Sir Oswald Moseley ten years previously, representing Ladywood.

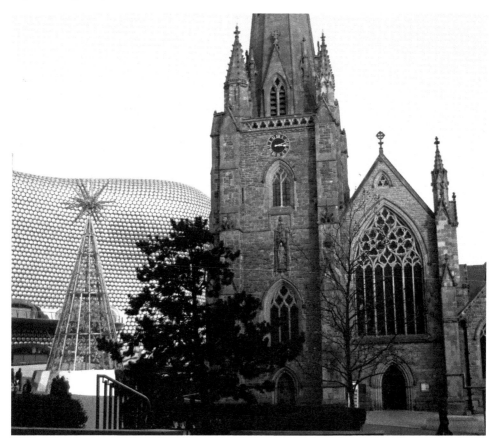

St Martins in the Bull Ring. (Courtesy of José Carlos Cortizo Pérez under Creative Commons 2.0)

Top of the Hill!

St Phillips was designed by local Warwickshire architect Thomas Archer, a pupil of Sir John Vanburgh. The cathedral's 'Wrenesque' style was endowed with fine stained-glass windows by William Morris. Birmingham's greatest painter, Burne Jones, designed the south transept window. He was baptised here, and his father lived close by. St Phillip's stands on the highest point in the city centre, a small green square between the two principle railway stations of Snow Hill and New Street. However, the new tram link doesn't pass this way – it goes to the High Street and Stephenson Street. The first time the city has seen them on the streets for sixty years! Some say they shouldn't have gone away in the first place.

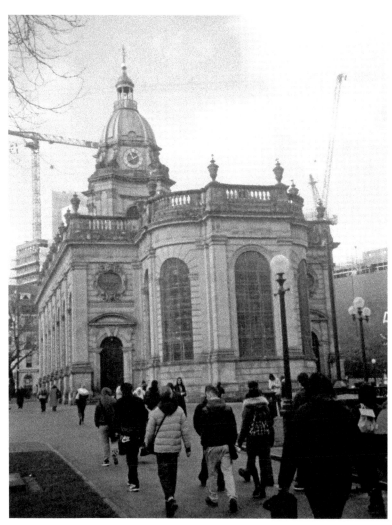

St Phillip's
Anglican
Cathedral.

The Chamberlains

Progress? But Chamberlain's legacy still stands. The much-talked-about 'Bauhaus' brutalist New Library succumbs to the wrecking ball, after it had been generally accepted in its short forty-year life. Much of the cities Victorian architecture has survived, although the most important buildings are Edwardian, such as the University of Birmingham at Edgbaston. This was originally founded in 1875 in nearby Edmund Street by Joseph Mason, who had some considerable wealth from manufacturing pens in Newtown. By 1896 it had become University College and with the support of Joseph Chamberlain, Lord Calthorpe and £50,000 form Andrew Carnegie, it was established as Birmingham's first university at Edgbaston. Mason College moved to Oxford in 1889, becoming Mansefield College.

Together with other liberal unionists, Joseph Chamberlain was the prime mover behind building the university on part of Lord Calthorpe's estate.

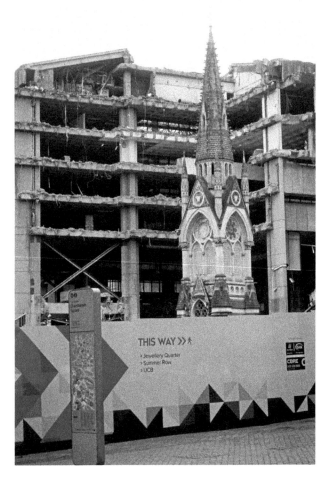

Chamberlain Memorial.

Jewellery Quarter

The Chamberlain clock was erected in the Jewellery Quarter in 1903 by some of his west Birmingham constituents, in recognition of his visit to South Africa as Secretary for the Colonies, at the important crossroads of Warstone Lane and Vyse Street/Frederick Street. Nearby are the old and new Assay Offices, founded in 1773 with Mathew Boulton's support – so no longer did precious metal have to be sent to London for hallmarking.

The new Assay Office is on the corner of Warstone Lane and Ladywood Queensway, on the edge of the Jewellery Quarter. From Newhall Street Bridge, just down from the striking Georgian parish church of St Paul's in Newtown (c. 1715), which forms a green square, and together with the businesses of Ludgate Hill inject a welcome splash of colour to this part of the city, along with the much-needed clean of the brickwork, revealing its warm hue.

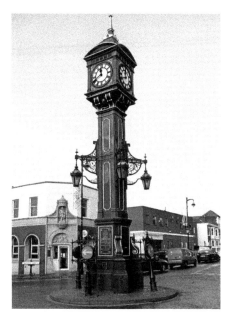

The Chamberlain clock. (Courtesy of John Lord under Creative Commons 2.0)

DID YOU KNOW?

Birmingham's Assay Office, now one of four in the UK and the busiest in Britain, has the anchor as its hallmark. Perhaps not unsurprisingly, Newhall Street, which links the heart of the city to Newtown, crosses the Birmingham Canal Navigations. Within the last year a larger Assay Office has been built adjacent to the old Birmingham Mint site.

There is still metal 'bashing' going on in these parts of inner Brum – On Mary Ann Street, a colonial give away in the shadow of the great GWR Snow Hill Viaduct. Here, too, is Birmingham's Rail Centre in miniature and, like the real thing, it doesn't run all the time – not on Mondays or Tuesdays except in school holiday time, otherwise Wednesday to Sunday from 10 a.m.

On Fredrick Street is the Pen Museum, a fascinating insight into calligraphy in this age of laptops. The Chamberlain's made their money in such a mundane manufactory near Smethwick, so in some ways Birmingham does owe its success more to the 'pen' than the 'sword'.

Another unusual visitor attraction is the Coffin Museum at the Newman Brothers Museum in Fleet Street, in the largely regenerated Quayside area – 'It's not what you might expect' – backing onto the University College of Birmingham in Lionel Street.

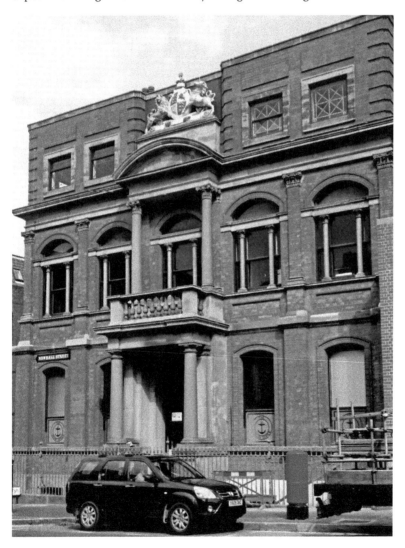

The Old
Assay Office,
Newhall Street.

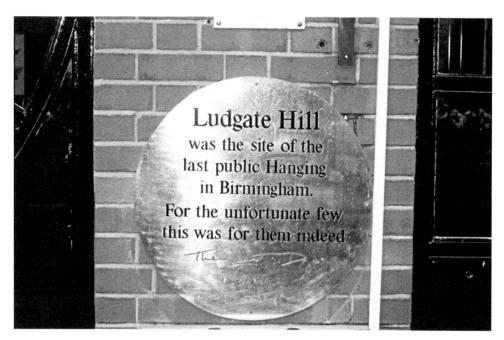

Above: Plaque in Ludgate Hill.

Right: St Paul's Church.

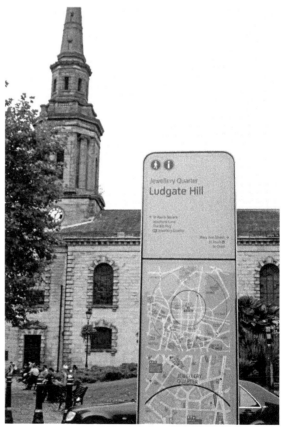

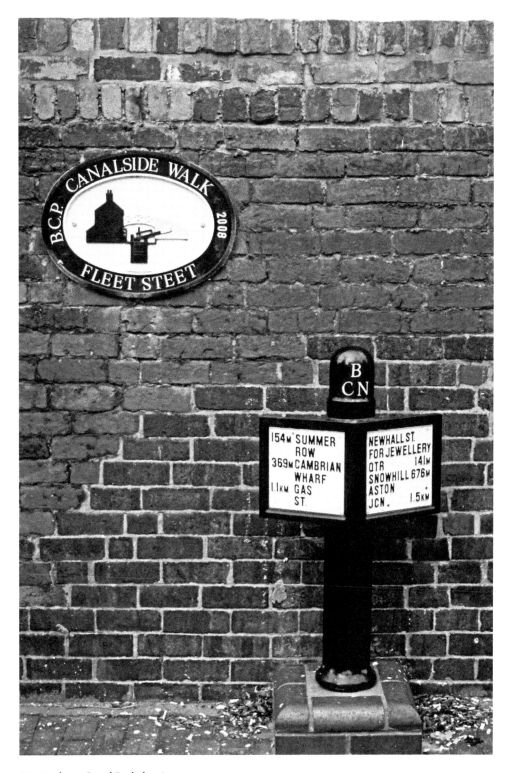

Birmingham Canal Path furniture.

Birmingham & Fazeley Canal

Lighthouse builder John Smeton from Devon was appointed as chief engineer to the Birmingham & Fazeley Canal Co. (BFCC) in 1783, to construct a link between Wednesbury and Coventry to supply coal. The Birmingham Canal Co. had tried to halt its construction, which involved three canal companies. The Coventry Canal Co. would build its extension to Fazeley near Tamworth. The new BFCC would then link to the Brindley-built Trent and Mersey at Fradley, thus enabling swifter transport of coal and other raw materials into the city and beyond. This arrangement was called the 'Coleshill Agreement'.

Staffordshire blue brick was the original builders' material, patched in porous red and erratically topped in shiny red. The 2008 renovation of Quayside brought metrification to the towpath – not a common sight generally.

The Farmers Locks greatly delayed the transit of goods, so that by the 1840s a new direct cut was made – the Tame Valley Canal. It had thirteen locks at Perry Barr. Upon completion of the Birmingham & Coventry Canal in 1794, the new company renamed itself Birmingham Canal Navigations (BCN).

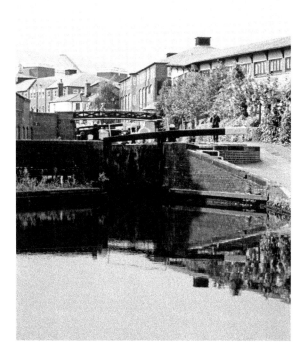

Farmers Lock built by John Smeaton of Devon.

Quayside

Invariably one will wander onto a towpath in this city with over 30 miles of canal, but to get across it in a narrowboat Farmers Locks (all thirteen of them) have to be encountered. The concrete and glass boom of the 1970s and '80s tried to make them even more subterranean than the seven bridges that cross the same stretch had done! New quayside apartments are part of Millennium regeneration by Farmers 'Old 13'.

Not quite a staircase from Aston Junction, more a cascade from Ladywood where the two main lines to Wolverhampton finally join. The rise/fall is 80 feet. The side ponds form mini passing places in an otherwise tight cut and the original town wharf was here. Only the Cambrian Wharf survives; many of the other basins were filled in for the Centenary Square development.

DID YOU KNOW?

The Post Office Tower is 500 feet high and was built between 1963 and 1965. It is still the tallest building in the city and can be seen from the M6 at Spaghetti Junction. It was designed by M. H. Bristow. Apart from housing BT microwave telecommunications, its home to the odd peregrine falcon.

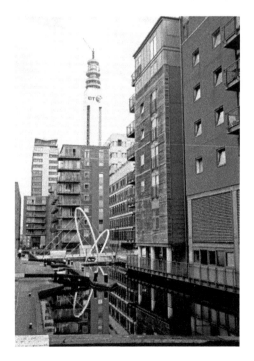

New city apartments on the former Cambrian Wharf site.

Old Turn Junction/Deep Cutting Junction – the Epitome of Birmingham's Venetian Image

This junction of four canals or branches lay at the heart of the canal/railway interchange. Malt houses, flour mills and tube works were concentrated in this part of Ladywood. With the Worcestershire Bar blocking connection in the Gas Street basin, the canals from the north focused here. The cast-iron roving bridges were manufactured by the Horseley Iron Works.

The lane that once ran off Broad Street to the Ozelles Street Wharf was called Brass House Parade (maybe it ought to be Brass Horse?). The LNWR Stour Valley Railway goods shed were by the side of the high level cut. The Midland Railway had its warehouses south of the Worcester Bar, off Gas Street basin.

Now overlooked by the Mail Box/Cube Centre, Gas Street basin is now fashionable. It is hard to picture the acute state of dereliction that our waterways were in in the 1960s and '70s. How could such an asset be so easily cast aside by such ignorance of the effort taken to build them and the vital role they have in draining the city – much more so than its rivers! Dozens of wharfs have been filled in, but the main routes have survived and now as at Ozelles it's a landscape asset.

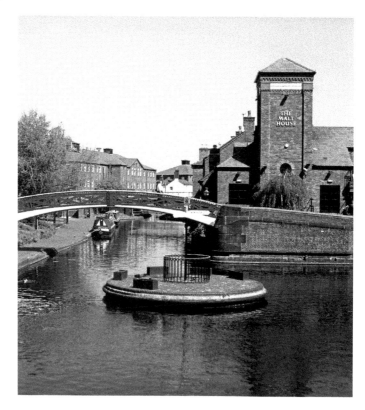

Old Turn Junction/ Deep Cutting Junction. (Courtesy of Elliot Brown under Creative Commons 2.0)

Roundhouses

Close to the National Indoor Arena is a Victorian arena for horses. Here the motive power for the canal boats were groomed and fed by the side of the main line – the Wolverhampton–Birmingham canal. The original James Brindley canal was built between 1768 and 1772, having twenty-nine locks in the 23.5 miles from Aldersley Junction (most in Wolverhampton). Once reaching Tipton Green, Telford's 'new' main line takes the direct route to Smethwick but has locks to encounter; whereas the 'old' main line contours to Oldbury, before they rejoin at the Stewart Aqueduct, Spon Lane. Smethwick, a municipal borough in Staffordshire, is often thought to be part of Birmingham – it never was and still isn't. It was the location of much manufacturing based in Birmingham.

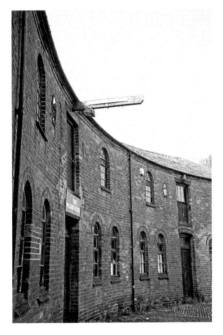

Stables for barges towing horses.

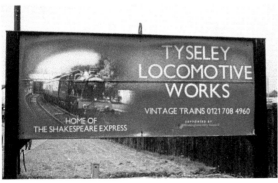

Tyseley Locomotive Works.

Tyseley

Once the GWR's locomotive works, today Tyseley is the site of London Midland maintenance depot near Tyseley Station, while the former roundhouse site is at the core of 'Vintage Trains' who run the *Shakespeare Express* to Stratford via Shirley and Earlswood Lakes. These steam hauled excursions are very popular in the summer months running at weekends, while a series of special UK-wide tours are programmed throughout the year. Rood Ashton Hall 4965 and Earl of Mount Edgecombe 5043 often head the Sunday Shakespeare specials to Stratford upon Avon. Oddly, the recreation of an extinct LNWR Bloomer 670 here was recently named *Prince George*.

When railways came to the area, roundhouses were built to 'stable' locomotives. Tyseley Depot had two, but sadly in the orgy of bulldozing Victoriana in the '60s and '70s these were demolished. Their turntable, now in the open air, does survive and has twenty-eight lines leading off it.

Other GWR locomotives have been restored including Kinlet Hall 4986, Clun Castle 7029, Pitchford Hall 4953, two Panier tank engines and also much work on LMS Patriot *Unknown Warrior* rebuild has been done at Tyseley. The main engine works (also ex-GWR) for the 45551 Patriot is being done at Llangollen, but as it is no longer attached to the national network, it seems a good chance we'll see this locomotive main line running from Tyseley in 2018.

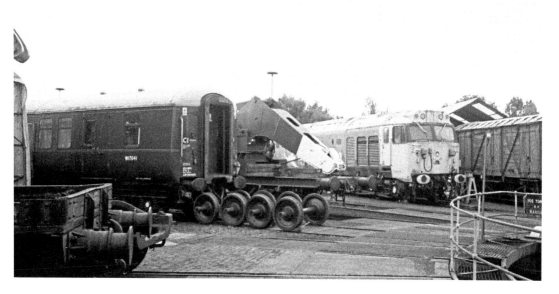

A turntable is all that remains of steam horse stables.

Civic Centre

Overlooking Chamberlain Square is the clock tower 'Big Brum'. It forms part of the Council House complex. Joseph Chamberlain was able to pay for the City's Art Gallery and Museum from the Corporations Gas Supply Department in 1881. The Free Public Art Gallery was opened by Richard Chamberlain, mayor – the commemorative stone carried the inscription 'By the gains of Industry we promote Art!' Designed by Yeoville Thomason at a cost of £163,000, it was completed in 1879 with an extension in 1885. It is now a Grade II-listed building. Queen Victoria even came to name the square.

As if a glint from 'Old Joe's' monocle, the front of the Council House provides a fine backdrop to the apparently unmarried Queen Victoria. The steps are the ultimate top of Hill Street from the River Rea, a direct line extending as Hurst Street to the river. To the left of Victoria Square is the modestly called Town Hall. Designed by J. A. Hanson and E. Welch, it is said to have been inspired by the Temple of Castor and Pollux. A Grade I-listed building, it underwent a £35-million renovation. It is over 182 years old and has seen first-night performances by Mendelssohn Elijah in 1846, the premier of

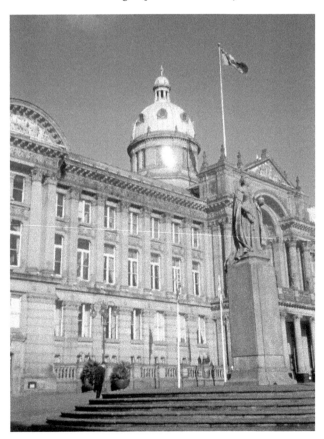

Council House opened by Queen Victoria.

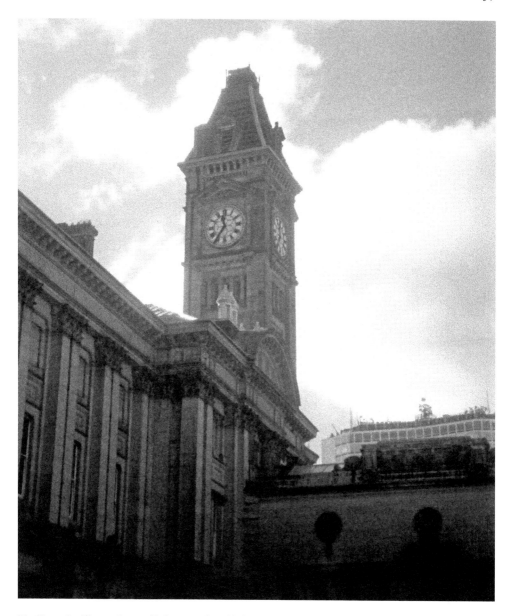

Big 'Brum' still stands to tell the time for all the citizens.

Dvorjak's 'Requiem' in 1891 and Edward Elgar's 'Dream of Gerontius' in 1900. Dickens, Dylan, the Beatles, Led Zeppelin and the Proclaimers have all appeared here.

Not the banks of the Nile, Mr Gormely's Iron Man has gone and the sphinx smiles down New Street. There were three statues at the top of the steps accompanying Old Queen Vic.

In 1993 Victoria Square was redesigned in collaboration with Dhruva Mistry. The upper and lower fountains were altered. The main sculptures were carved out of Darley Dale limestone and the bronze 'fluzzy in the Jacuzzi'. Now the reclining beauty is surrounded by cacti – a bed of thorns!?

Peeping over the skyline is the curved trapezoidal Betham Tower and the other blocks along the A38 expressway – Suffolk Queensway in the direction of the uninspiring Cube and Mailbox.

Behind Brums Council House are a few Gothic gems: the School of Art, the Birmingham and Midland Institute, and the University College of Birmingham, Lionel Street.

The BMI was founded in 1854 by the Act of Parliament for the 'Diffusion and advancement of Science, Literature and Art amongst all classes of persons resident in Birmingham and Midland Counties'. Charles Dickens was an early president. It contains the Birmingham Library of 100,000 books, 6,000 biographies and a music library. John Lee, a button manufacturer of Snow Hill, founded the collection in 1779. Joseph Priestley, pioneering chemist and discover of oxygen, reorganised the private lending library in 1781.

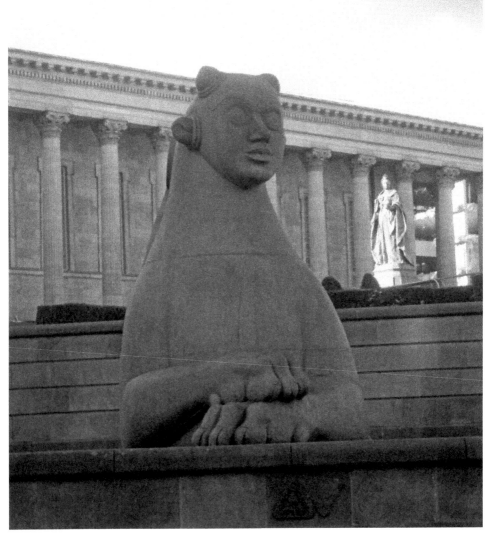

A modern sculpture in Victoria Square in front of the Council House.

In 1797 it was housed in a purpose-built location in Union Street near Martineau Place, before the days of Corporation Street – that was another Chamberlain legacy of 1879. Since 1899 the library has been housed in Margate Street. The BMI has an active study, lecture, concert and debate programme every month.

DID YOU KNOW?

The Birmingham and Midland Institute has been in existence since 1854, founded by Act of Parliament for the 'Diffusion and Advancement of Science, Literature and Art amongst all classes of Persons resident in Birmingham and Midland Counties.' Rural members pay a lower subscription fee as they have to travel further to the Institute.

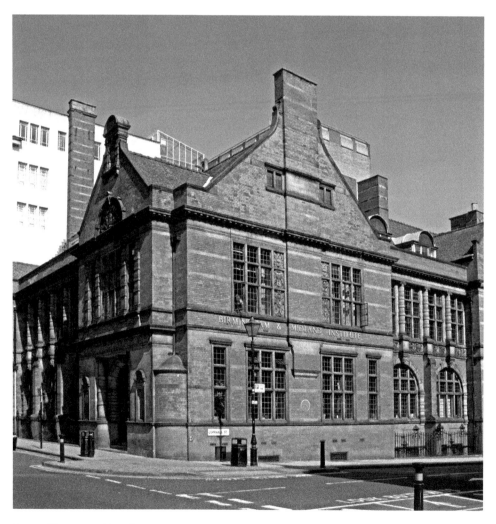

Seats of learning old and new. (Courtesy of Tony Hisgett under Creative Commons 2.0)

Down to the River:
Victoria Square to Sherlock Street

It is unusual to find a memorial to a Lancashire Quaker, as in John Bright Street off Hill Street, the reformer for the Corn Laws and supporter of the Reform Act 1867 as an MP. He was MP for the city of Durham in 1843–47. As co-founder of the Anti-Corn Law League, he raised over £8 million (in today's money). He would have known Sir Robert Peel, who also wanted to abolish these protectionist laws. He became a minister and lord rector of Glasgow University and would have known Joseph Chamberlain, who upon giving a rectoral address at Glasgow in 1897, vowed that Birmingham would 'have a University of its own'.

Several Quaker or Unitarian families gave the city firm foundations, from the Cadburys, Attwood, Dawson, and Dixon Collins to the Chamberlains.

The view form John Bright Street, which, despite the sign 'Mailbox', the New Street station (now rebranded Grand Central) has replaced the old 1960s square-edged Birmingham Shopping Centre. The proud refurbished Rotunda Bull Ring Tower survived

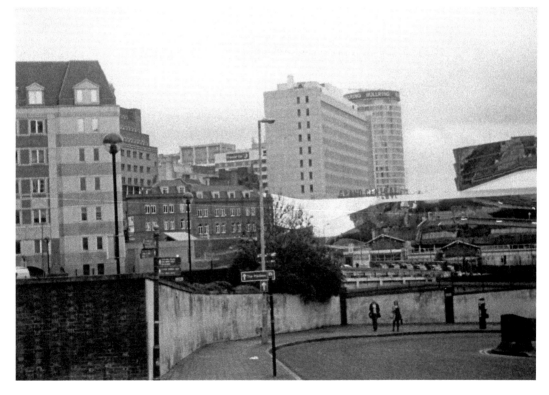

Down John Right Street.

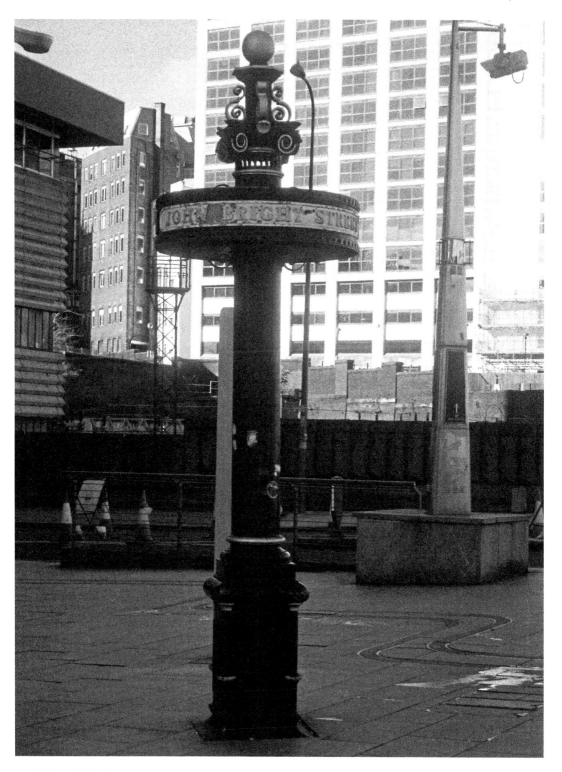

Down Right Street.

IRA bombings in the 1980s and reminds us that a few concrete buildings are worth keeping. It is a landmark in the city centre. I wonder how long the slab block will last before it is torn down? The Mailbox is a good example of refurbishment but it is behind us – 'under' the Suffolk Street Queensway (A38) dual carriageway.

Chamberlain Tower at Birmingham University's Edgbaston campus has the world's largest free-standing clock tower. Its design was based upon St Mark's Square in Venice – a city often alluded to in another comparison: its canals.

Cultural Quarter

At the highest point of Queensway is the Pagoda, similar in design to the Earl of Shrewsbury's at Alton Towers. It is now overshadowed by the Beta/Betham Tower. At 430 feet high it was designed to have forty-four floors but was reduced to forty. Designed by Ian Simpson Co., it sits on only 1⅛ acres. The lower portion is occupied by the 'Radisson

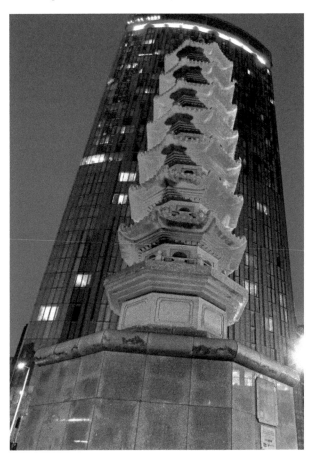

Pogoda, Queensway. (Courtesy of Scott Macpherson under Creative Commons 2.0)

Hotel', while the rest are 156 luxury apartments. Somehow it won the RIBA housing design award! I suspect they wanted to try to overtop the GPO Tower at 500 feet. They certainly did beat the Alpha Tower.

Looking down Smallbrook Ringway towards New Street and the Debenhams corner of the Bull Ring shopping area, Chinatown lays between Hurst Street and Dean Street.

Wrottesley Street – named after a Staffordshire lord – echoes the old Brum and is near the Central Markets on Southside. They are as large as New Street/Pallasadas and the Bull Ring Mall put together.

Hurst Street is home to the Birmingham Hippodrome, built in 1899, but has had several facelifts and is now the home for the Royal Ballet. Under the directorship of Matthew Bourne, who choreographed and produced the first all-male *Swan Lake*, it has gained an international reputation.

On the adjacent corner are the only remaining back to back 'slums' in the city – now owned by the National Trust for the nation.

Opposite the Hippodrome is the 'Old Fox' theatre bar. Two other Birmingham theatres that have some longevity are close by – the Alexandra Rep and the Electric Theatre in Station Street next to the Old Rep. The 'Old Fox' was one of the first public places where gay and lesbian people were able to meet free from ridicule and intolerance.

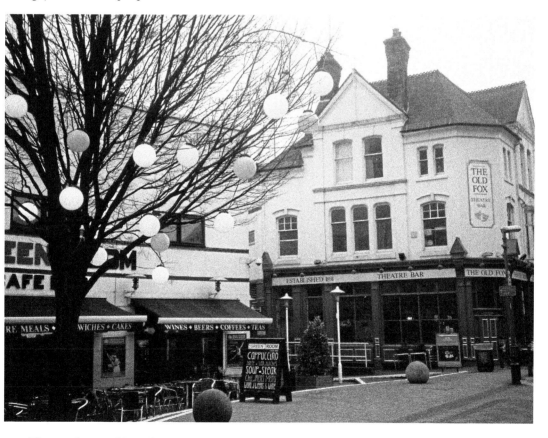

Theatre Quarter, Hurst Street.

Back to Backs

The Back to Backs date from 1840 and are in a courtyard of eleven houses still retaining their original grates (open daily except Mondays). At the other end of Hurst/Sherlock Street are the still-remaining Victorian street corner pubs in impressive red Gothic brick. Close to the River Rea is the Irish Quarter.

Birmingham can lay claim to the largest St Patrick's Day Parade in the world outside Dublin and New York. It is always a welcome splash of colour in March.

Hurst Street is the centre of colour in May when the city's Gay Pride weekend occurs. This features the parade of floats and over a weeks' worth of arts events at various venues including the MAC in Cannon Hill Park by the side of the River Rea

Apparently not only does the M5 go to Brum but the C5 does too. This is the NCR post in the Village. Every Whit May, Birmingham has one of the largest LGBT Pride parades. The well-known Nightingales dance club and Missing Bar can be found in the Village. A programme of events takes place at other venues too, in the past at the MAC and the Custard Factory.

NCR 5 enters the city at Frankley, follows the Rea Valley from Longbridge to Gooch Street, where it departs the river up Hurst Street. It zigzags across to Centenary Square to join the Wolverhampton High Level Canal going north-west, leaving the city at Winson Green. Three other NCR trails enter the city: 525/533 Tame Valley with 534 Sutton Coldfield via Castle Bromwich looping back to 533. Over the last ten years cycling has grown by over 75 per cent in the city and is becoming cycle city.

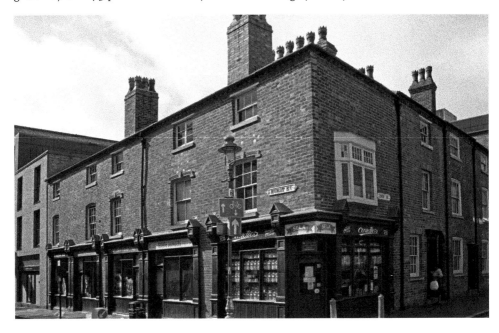

National Trust preserved Back to Backs. (Courtesy of Tony Hisgett under Creative Commons 2.0)

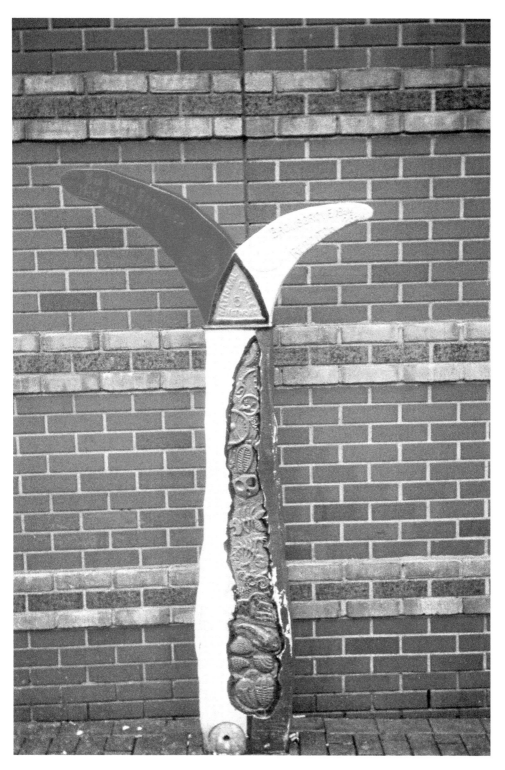

C5 National Cycle Trail goes through the gay village.

Hurst Street

Halfway down Hurst Street at the junction of Skinner Lane (not named after Frank) there is an allusion to the meat market that preceded the modern wholesale General Market now occupying Southside, between Barford Street, Digbeth High Street and Pershore Street. Road names can be revealing – South Rea Street gives a clue to Birmingham's river. It flows through Digbeth largely underground; its course heads north-east to Vauxhall and its confluence with Staffordshire's Tame at Nechells.

Some of the city's last remaining terraced row pubs have survived the Blitz and redevelopment on Birchall Street. They exhibit some of the finest Gothic architecture still to be seen, like bookends marking the former terraces

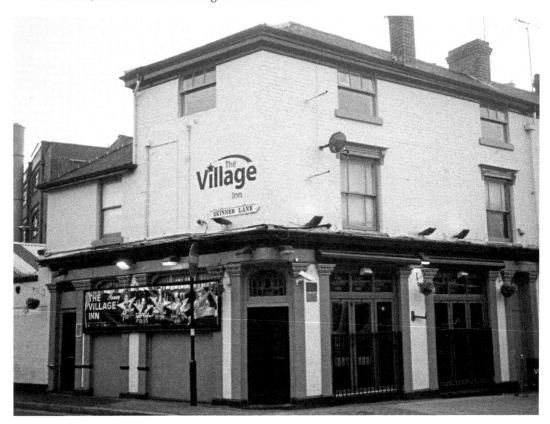

The Village Inn, Hurst Street.

Southern Suburbs

By 1832 Deritend and Bordesley were absorbed into the Borough of Birmingham and it had got parliamentary representation. Civic responsibilities for public health, education and housing took a while for the new Corporation to grapple with. Deritend still has the first branch library built in the 1860s on Heath Mill Lane, close by is the custard factory built by Alfred Bird by the River Rea. Over 1,000 were employed by Bird's.

Renovation and redevelopment of the custard factory began in 1992 to establish an arts and media hub here with studios, galleries, shops and theatre space employing 300 to grow to 1,000. But then we had the crash/recession/austerity. It has been the focal point for several festival events involving local community groups.

Floodgate Street runs parallel to the River Rea, hidden between light engineering factories still working today. To continue tracing the Rea, a clue is given in River Street, which still retains a complete row of domestic architecture from the 1850s.

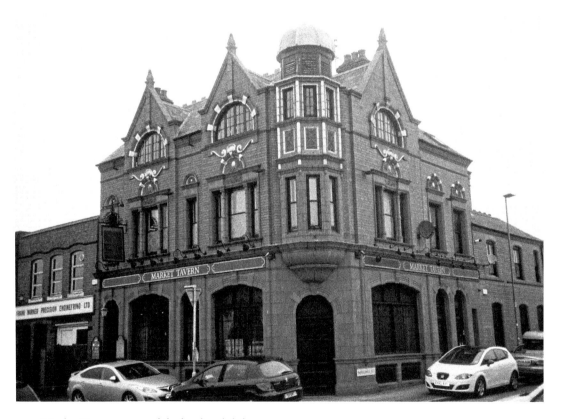

Market Tavern – one of the bookends left.

Rhubarb and Custard

This image shows part of the renovated custard factory buildings on River Rea south side, whereabouts Heath Mill was located, one of nearly thirty sited on the Rea or its tributaries.

One of the new galleries is called 'The Rhubarb' to go with the Custard. Two of the buildings are painted red and yellow, the colours of Bird's packaging. One could say it's been tarted up since his day!

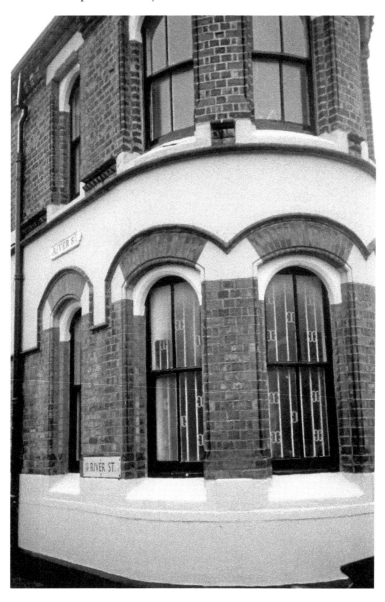

River Street –
River Rea.

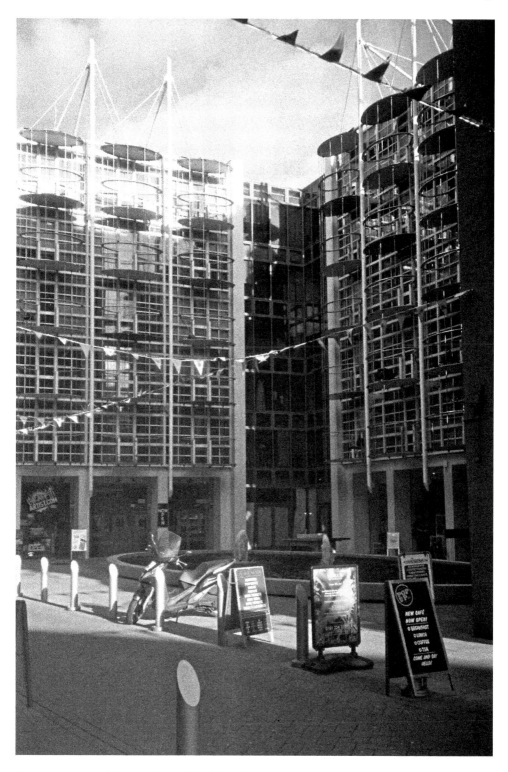

Renovated custard factory, South Side, River Rea.

Middle Earth – Tolkien Country

J. R. R. Tolkien's dragon? This fine specimen is on the east wall of the custard factory and appears to be about to launch over the River Rea and swoop under the Digbeth Viaduct. Tolkien favoured a section of the River Cole at Hall Green. Sarehole Mill, once owned by Matthew Boulton, was an inspiring haunt for the younger Tolkien. Close by is Moseley Bog, which has amazingly been protected by the Wildlife Trust. The inspiration for *The Hobbit* is claimed to have come from his boyhood escapades, and the wooded nature of the valley set his mind to create the ancient forests of the Lord of the Rings. The mill is the best surviving example of watermills of which there are over forty-five on Birmingham's rivers, and is managed by the City Museum Trust – producing freshly ground flour most Wednesdays and Sundays. There are only two working mills remaining.

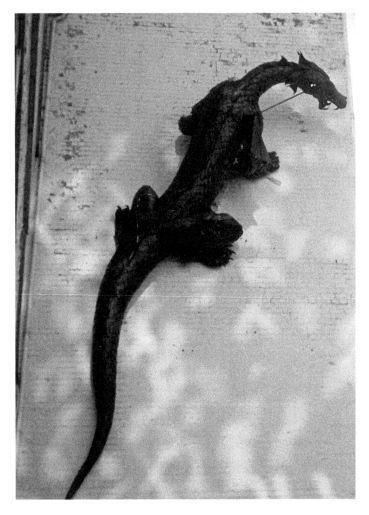

Dragon on the east wall of the custard factory overlooking the River Rea.

Twin Towers

Edgbaston, to the west of the city centre, has Tolkien's 'Two Towers', off Monument Road. The construction of the 85-mile-long Elan Aqueduct gave rise to the Lower Edgbaston Waterworks Pumping Station and dates from the late 1890s. The nearby surface reservoir, formerly known as Rotton Lake, is a feed supply to the BCN network and was built in 1829 by Thomas Telford, and contains 300 million gallons. This area was known as Rotton Park. Perriots Tower, built as an observatory in 1758, stood originally in open parkland at 524 feet and is approximately 200 feet high. Together with the pump house tower, they provided Tolkien with the title of his second 'Rings' book – *The Two Towers* – as he worked at the 'Ivory Towers' of Birmingham University.

Perriots folly on Waterworks Road is visible from Edgbaston Pump House. The area was part of the Calthorpe estate, parts of which began to be sold off in 1786. The area known as Islington (Five Ways) was at the edge of Calthorpe Park, guarded by toll houses on the Hagley and Harborne roads. By 1820 George, Frederick and Calthorpe roads were laid out between the Harborne and Wheeleys Road. At 524 feet above sea level, it affords good views over the city centre and only 20 feet higher than 'Five Ways'. Occasionally open to the public, it is used as a community arts exhibition space. Due south is Edgbaston Botanical Gardens.

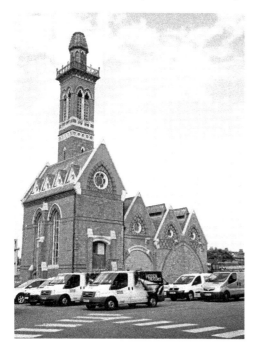 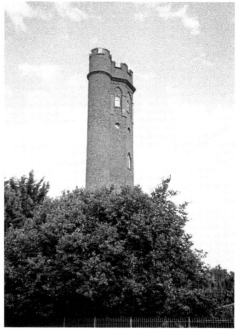

Above left: One of the Twin Towers.

Above right: The Edgbaston Waterworks pumping station.

Sarehole Mill

The River Cole rises on Headley Heath and has flowed 9 miles to reach Hall Green and Sarehole Mill. It flows to the east of Central Birmingham, through Sparkhill, Smallheath, and Yardley to Stetchford. Below Alum Rock it swings east flowing parallel to the Tame, which it later joins beyond Coleshill, bringing its 22-mile course to an end at Blythe End. The valley is a linear park for 12 miles from Yardley Wood, accompanied by a walking/cycle route.

Sarehole Mill dates back to 1542. By 1756 it had been leased by Mathew Boulton, who converted it to roll sheet metal until the late 1760s, when he moved production to his new Soho manufactory in Handsworth.

DID YOU KNOW?

J. R. R. Tolkien's haunt by Sarehole/Moseley Bog is in the second longest valley that falls mainly within the city – the Cole Valley. It was the location of Sarehole Mill. Also with a tall tower, its chimney was built by Matthew Boulton around 1780 when he replaced the watermill with a steam-powered mill.

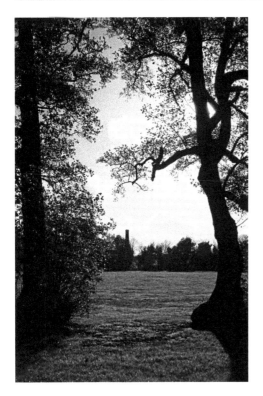

A watermill was built in the Cole Valley, used by Boulton who then replaced it with a steam engine.

Triffid Gate

Birmingham Botanical Gardens date from 1830, designed by J. C. Louden. They were added to in 1870 with the building of a bandstand and glasshouses. By 1901 most of the Calthorpe estate had been made almost entirely residential. Edgbaston Park was originally landscaped by Capability Brown and remains today in the Chad Valley as a belt of green land, mostly as a golf course.

Loudon was known for his gardening encyclopaedia produced in 1822, which was the first of its kind. Birmingham Horticultural Society successfully purchased the land south of Westbourne Road, from John Aspley, which had a good mixture of soil, loam, bog and clay. The acclimatisation of foreign plants was seen as part of the botanical science he wanted the garden to foster. Not until 1890 was a rock garden added. With some of the glasshouses over 100 years old, the Birmingham Botanical Gardens are currently fundraising to replace them.

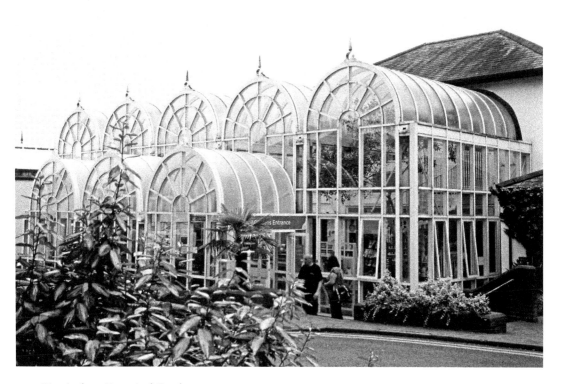

Birmingham Botanical Gardens.

Land of Rhododendrons

Overlooking Edgbaston Reservoir, the Dhamma Talaka Peace Pagoda was built in 1998 and adds a sparkle to the south-west of Central Birmingham. It is modelled on the Shwedagon Pagoda in Burma. Another unexpected group also found near the reservoir is T. S. Vernon – one of three sea cadet units based in the city. There are three rowing clubs also based on the lake and a sailing club – the old joke about the Birmingham Navy is far from the truth.

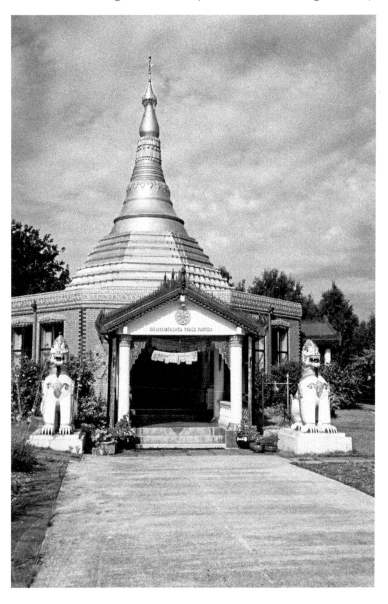

Splendid Dhamma Talaka Peace Pagoda, overlooking Edgbaston Reservoir.

Oldest Church in the City

It is recorded in the Domesday Book as 'Gerlei' or 'Yerdeley'. The hazel stream, the River Cole, originates in early British days. A Saxon charter of 972 refers to it as a boundary – Maerebroc – between Worcestershire and Warwickshire. Yardley grew up around St Edburghas.

The parish of Yardley was one of the largest in Worcestershire before it was incorporated into the city in the massive expansion of 1911. St Edburgha was a Saxon princess, granddaughter of King Alfred. The Greswoldes were lords of the manor. Inside are works

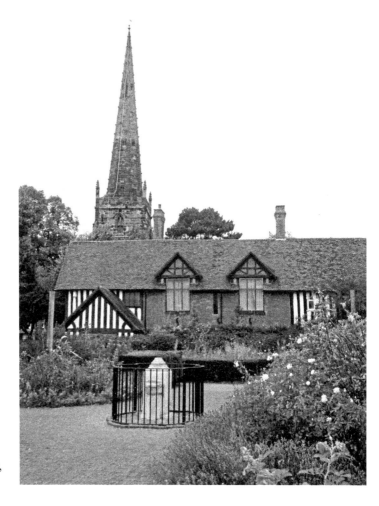

St Edburghas, Yardley,
founded in 972.

of the Birmingham School of Art. Thomas Est was governor of Kenilworth Castle in the county of Warwick. His tomb is in the Gilby Chapel.

Edburgha later became prioress at Pershore Abbey and Yardley was one of its estates. Initially interred at Pershore upon her death, it is believed that some remains are buried in front of the altar in the church. Can you find the Rose and Pomegranate? Yardley District Council didn't locate their council house here but at Sparkhill on the Stratford Road (A34), as they anticipated housing expansion in the western part of the district nearest Birmingham pre-1911.

The 175-foot spire dominates the small close; no through traffic is permitted today. The half-timbered Yardley Trust School is said to date back to the late 1400s, becoming the home of the earlier Priory School established around 1250 by the monks of Maxstoke Abbey (further down the Cole Valley) where the River Blythe meets it.

DID YOU KNOW?

Overnight in 1911 the newly incorporated districts of Yardley, Kings Norton and Northfield 'hopped' from Worcestershire to Warwickshire on OS maps – as Birmingham was always part of the latter.

The Oldest Surviving King Edward VI School: Kings Norton

St Nicholas Church goes back to Norman times, but its spire was acquired in the 1400s. In its shadow is the half-timbered King Edward VI School. The scholar Thomas Hall was its head teacher during the Civil War, seeing the Royalist armies pass through the village twice, removing lead off the church roof to make bullets. A poet and writer, he collected many books despite much opposition to his lectures and Puritan views – 'Brown bread and the Gospel' was his motto. Today his rare book collection is kept in the City Central Library, itself the largest public library in the UK and home to the world's largest collection of Shakespearian works.

The local community have raised the wherewithal to restore the old school building for community use and, despite recent vandalism by lead thieves, can feel rightly proud of their winning the BB2 Restoration award in 2004.

The long six-bay Tudor merchant house dates to 1492, built for the wool merchant Humphrey Rotsey. It was here adjacent to the Saracens Head that Queen Henrietta (wife of Charles I) lodged in July 1643 on her way from York with troops. The other royal connection that Kings Norton has isn't so obvious. Close to the River Rea and the junction

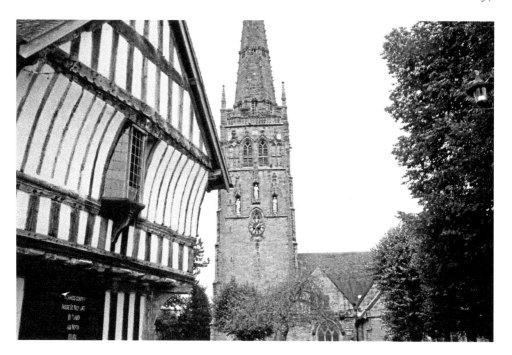

Kings Norton Tudor merchant house and impressive Norman church tower.

of the Worcester–Birmingham canal and Stratford–Birmingham canal was the Kings Norton Mint. Sovereign Road is a token gesture to its existence.

Birmingham Mints had produced coins and medals for several colonies including British West Africa, India and for UK circulation.

DID YOU KNOW?

Revd W. Audrey lived in Kings Norton. He was the author of the Thomas the Tank Engine stories set on the fictitious island of Sodor – the ancient name associated with the Isle of Man. His books were very popular in the 1950s and '60s and again in the 1980s and '90s when the stories were animated for TV.

Aston Park, Aston on Tame

This lovely avenue of trees forms the northern walk to the hall from the city centre. 'East' town has some of the most complete Victorian houses in terraces in its new town to the north and west of Aston Hall.

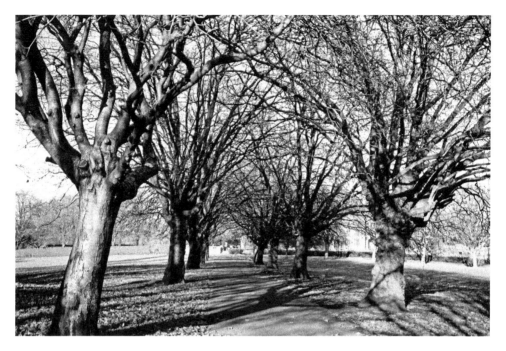

Western Avenue of beeches to Aston Hall.

Aston Manor

Aston Hall is a fine Jacobean mansion, dating from 1618 to 1635 and built by Sir Thomas Holte. Grade I listed, it is furnished to portray key historical periods from the Civil War. Cannon ball damage inside is evidenced on the staircase. Holte held it for King Charles only to be outnumbered forty to 1200! The king stayed here before the Battle of Edgehill. The Holtes were forced to sell their prized home and James Watt resided here, as did his sons between 1819 and 1849.

Some of the 330-acre park was rented off to Samuel Potter. A new west lodge was built giving James Jr access to Soho manufactory. Part of the estate was developed as Aston New Town. The Great Pool was in Staffordshire, part of Handsworth. After the death of James Watt Jr, the estate was offered to Birmingham Corporation but they didn't have powers of purchase in another local authority. In 1856 the hall and 43 acres were acquired by Aston Hall and Park Co. for the benefit of the 'working classes'.

In 1858 Queen Victoria visited Birmingham. It had been a borough for twenty years and was growing – the population was 182,992 people. Aston Manor wanted to be a municipal authority but its bigger neighbour objected.

When the queen opened the park for the public, only the deposit had been paid to acquire the hall and the immediate gardens. Even by 1863 Birmingham had acquired purchasing powers, but hadn't raised all the money, so was jolted to do so when the queen wrote expressing her surprise that with so many rich people in the area that the money hadn't been raised; it was fully purchased the next year.

DID YOU KNOW?

Aston (East Town) was founded on the River Tame in Saxon times and was in the control of the Holte family from the Middle Ages up until 1819.

Birmingham (or West town) was jealous of its near neighbour, as it encroached the boundary with back to backs of the Lozelles district – not of such a high standard as those in Aston. Joseph Chamberlain fought against the 'back to backs' being built. In 1841 the population was around 3,000 and by 1890 55,000! It has some of the best surviving mid-Victorian domestic architecture on the roads named after its early developers – Whitehead.

Whitehead Road schools were influenced by the architectural style of Aston Hall. They date from 1881 and demonstrate Aston's civic pride. This new town moved the centre of Aston to the west. The Expressway (A38) would cut old and new in half. A town hall was built at the junction of Witton Road and Albert Road, all in anticipation of Aston's bid for borough status in 1872 – it was given the consolation of an urban district. The King Edward VI Grammar School on Albert Road and the more generous Victoria Road houses were complimented by public baths. The New Town had six new schools, including one for the deaf, and a library, and also two new churches: St James on Whitehead Road and Six Ways Baptist Church.

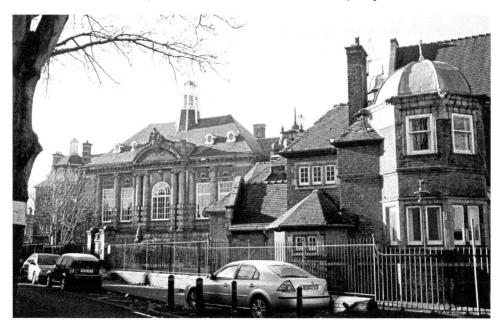

Whitehead Road schools.

Aston on Tame

The striking octagon cupola of Aston Manor Borough town hall on Albert Road and Witton Road. It was to be short lived as, along with Handsworth, Eardington, Kings Norton, Northfield Urban District Council and Yardley District Council, they all succumbed to Birmingham's expansion in 1911. Six years previously the city had been given a diocese separate from Lichfield and Coventry.

Aston's former town hall was built in 1872, finally gaining borough status in 1903 with a population of 80,000. It was the Villa Cross Wesleyan Chapel that formed the football club of 1875. Two cup semi-finals were played here in 1890 and 1896 by which year they had won the league twice.

The present stadium is between Aston Hall and the River Tame. It is possible to follow the River Trent's largest tributary from Nechells, Witton, Perry Bridges, Perry Barr, Hamstead and Sandwell Valley. It drains most of the Black Country to the north of the city and receives all of Birmingham's rivers as tributaries at Hams Hall via the Rivers Rea, Cole and Blythe.

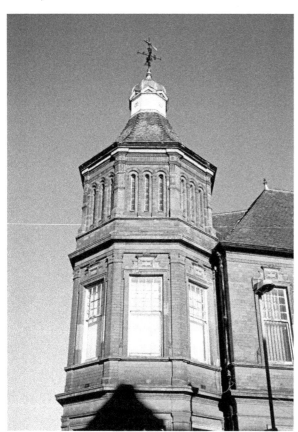

Symbol of civic pride soon to be dashed by big brother.

Aston University

The year 2016 is Aston's fiftieth anniversary as a fully independent university. It began as the University Technology College in 1951. Its roots were in the School of Metallurgy in 1875. In 1938 the Costa Green site was acquired after 'slum' clearance of many back to backs, but building was delayed due to the Second World War. Now part of an ever-expanding redeveloped the east side Millennium Point. Birmingham City University and Metropolitan College are adjacent. Aston's faculties still focus on sciences, computing and mathematics. It can claim to have built the world's longest laser among other achievements.

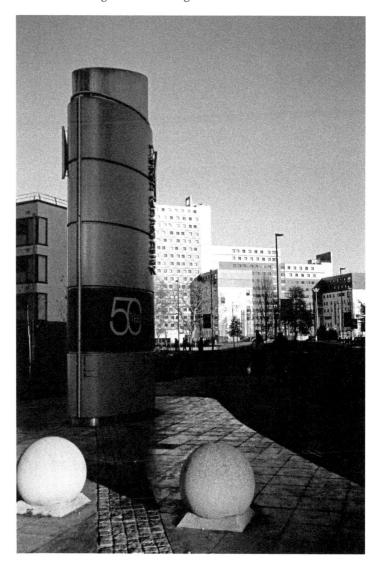

Sculpture celebrating the fiftieth anniversary of Aston University.

James Watt Engine, Aston Expressway / Middleway

By the early 1700s Newcomen's atmospheric engine was working successfully in the Black Country coalfield. Mathew Boulton had offered James Watt the backing and facilities to improve the early steam engine. His design was 75 per cent more efficient and went into production in 1776.

This Watt engine dates from 1817 and was employed at the Netherton Ironworks of W. M. Grazebrook. Although this is huge, the world's largest working engine is the Smethwick engine, formerly employed from 1779 pumping water for the locks on the Old Main Line canal. It is now housed in the Think Tank Science and Industry Museum at Millennium Point. The Newcomen engine has been faithfully rebuilt in working order at the Black Country Museum, Tipton Green, Staffordshire.

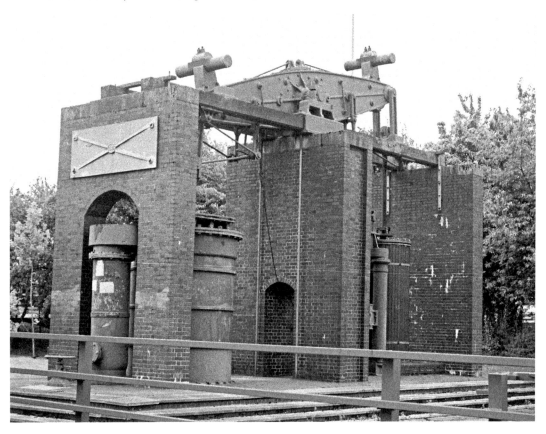

James Watt Engine, Aston Expressway/Middleway.

St Michael's, Soho Hill

The striking spire of St Michael's at the top of Soho Hill is seen from the Sandwell Valley. It was built as Handsworth and grew in the 1800s, providing Staffordshire with much-needed rate revenue. Handsworth was an important division in the county; it was a major part of the ancient Hundred of Offlow – a hint to King Offa. It was the basis of a large Poor Law Union covering most of the south-east part of the Black Country.

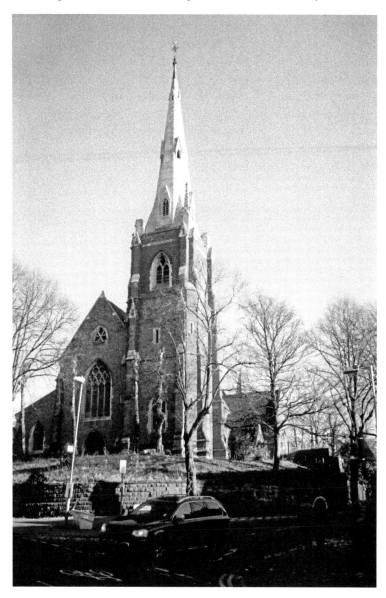

Symbol of expanding Handsworth, Staffordshire.

Handsworth Under the Sun/Soho Hill, Villa Road, St Michael's Road

Since the civil disruption in the 1980s local communities have made a determined effort to heal rifts and the civic sculpture on the A41 (Holyhead Road) at its junction with the B4144 near to Gib Heath and Lozells. At this junction, on three sides facing each other, are a mosque, a chapel and an Anglican church.

The unique steel sculpture declares 'under the sun our shadow points in the same direction'. Certainly Josiah Wedgwood, who campaigned against slavery, would have understood clearly. Close by is Soho House. Mathew Boulton, a fellow member of the Lunar Society, was a humanitarian as well as an entrepreneur. He would have admired the metalwork as well as the aphorism. At the top of Soho Hill on the important Holyhead Road from London it is close to striking St Michael's Church with its tall spire facing Mathew Murdoch's Soho House (now run by Birmingham City Museums Trust).

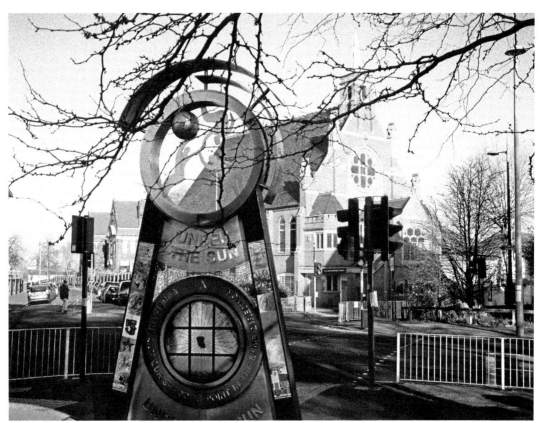

Handsworth Under the Sun.

Soho House, Soho Hill, Handsworth

Mathew Boulton's Soho House is opposite St Michael's Parish Church, Handsworth, Staffordshire. Born in 1728, he benefitted from a grammar school education. His father was a skilled silversmith. Together with John Fothergill, they established the Soho Manufactory in 1766 and also the Soho Mint, both of which survived until 1868. The first coins minted by steam press were produced here, including the infamous 'cartwheel two pence' in 1797 during George III's reign. It was the largest copper coin ever struck (weighing 2 ounces).

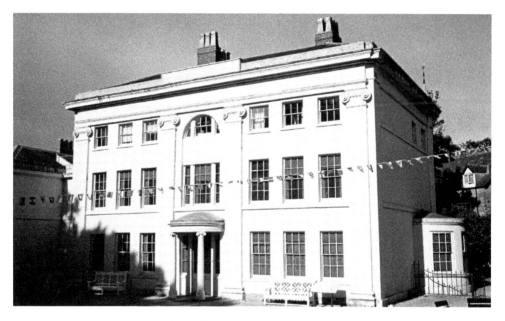

Matthew Boulton's home, Handsworth.

Old Mint / Birmingham Mint, Icknield Street

In 1862 Ralph Heaton & Sons established the Birmingham Mint, the largest private mint in the world, producing coinage for many overseas governments including France, Russia, Italy and the Commonwealth. It was located on Icknield Street, Hockley, until 2003 when it was sold. Number 1 The Mint is all that a visitor can presently find that acknowledges the existence of the Birmingham Mint. In 2003 it was sold to an Indian company and 'asset stripped'.

Ironically Birmingham's new Assay Office has been built across the Warstone Road junction, in Staffordshire blue brick, also on Icknield Street. It has been greatly enlarged since moving from Newhall Street and is the UK's largest Assay Office today.

Some of the rarest Victorian pennies are those minted by Heatons in 1912 and 1918 – the 'H' mark indicates these coins. Some pennies had holes in the middle – these were for British West Africa. Most of the peoples of the Gold Coast (Ghana), Nigeria, Gambia and Sierra Leonne didn't wear garments with pockets and so strung coins around their necks.

Birmingham's twenty-first-century Assay Office is on the new Ladywood Middleway, as the realigned Icknield Road is now called. The Jewellery Quarter provides the Assay Office with plenty of silver to stamp the anchor upon.

Boulton's partnership with Murdoch and Watt produced a dynamic industrial period of innovation not only for Birmingham but for the UK. Matthew Boulton was a founder member of the Lunar Society. He was a keen amateur scientist along with Erasmus Darwin, Joseph Priestly, Josiah Wedgwood, Samual Galton, James Kier, William Small, John Whitehurst and others. It existed until 1813 when many of the original members had died or left. In 1990 Dame Rachael Waterhouse reformed the society.

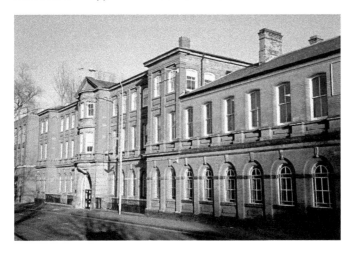

Birmingham Old Mint, formerly the oldest in the world.

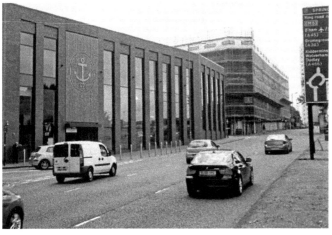

New Assay Office – the biggest in Britain.

Birmingham Museum service have recreated Mathew Boulton's study laboratory from Soho House, at the Think Tank Science and Industry Museum. Boulton began with inlaid steel buckles, buttons and watch chains, before going on to invent a technique for reproducing classical works of art in metal. He manufactured the machinery for producing coins, telescopes and astronomical clocks. He was generous and open minded, hosting the Lunar Society at Soho House. The house is open to the public between Easter and October, furnished as it was in Boulton's day. Many cultural activities are run here.

The City Museum has produced an informative leaflet: 'Mathew Boulton's Birmingham: A City Centre Walk and Lunar Society in 18th century Birmingham.'

On Foundary Road, Smethwick is the main part of Boulton and Watts's steam engine works of 1796. It is owned by Avery Scales today. Close by is William Murdoch's cottage.

It was due to Murdoch's experimentation with coal gas retorts that the Smethwick Foundary was the first factory in the world to be lit by gas in 1802.

DID YOU KNOW?

The world's first steam-pressed, die-cut coins were produced by Mathew Boulton and Co. Ltd during the reign of George III. These were mainly copper coins – halfpenny, penny and the unusual twopence. The size and weight of the twopence was such that it was called a 'Cartwheel' and was so unpopular it was only minted for two years.

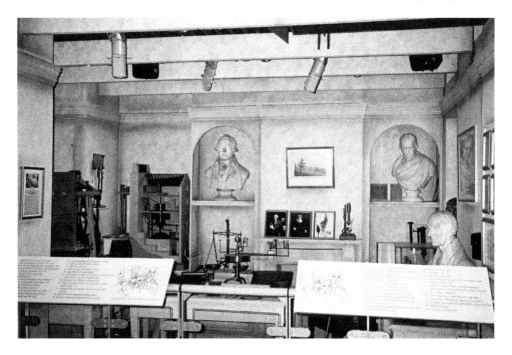

Recreated study/scientific room of Mathew Boulton.

St Mary's Parish Church, Handsworth

A lovely red-sandstone church with an ancient tower at 365 feet, St Mary's is at least 560 years old and was built on the road to Hampstead (which was part of Staffordshire). Hampstead was Perry Barr's civic centre until 1931, now situated opposite Handsworth Park. Boulton, Murdoch and Watt were all buried here. Fine busts of them by skilled sculptors are Handsworth's proud legacy; Flaxman shows Boulton plainly, while Chantry produced Watt's statue and Murdoch's bust. They died respectively in 1809, 1819 and 1839.

Handsworth was itself added to the city of Birmingham in 1911, previously a huge urban district in Staffordshire. It gave its name to the division of Offlow hundred, which covered most of the Black Country including Wednesbury, West Bromwich, Smethwick and Harborne.

The park is a lovely spot with a mature lake, sadly bisected by the Tame Valley railway line, largely in a cutting.

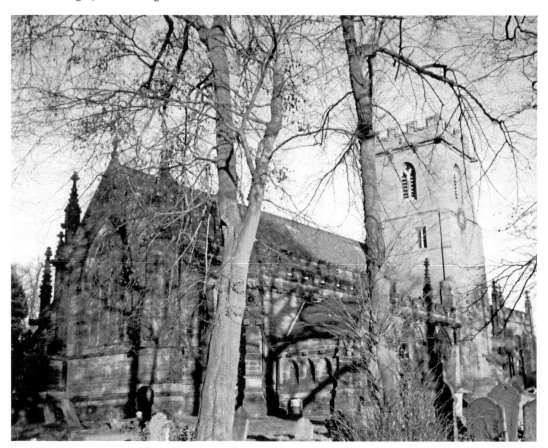

St Mary's Church, Handsworth.

Lovely Lozells

On Heathfield Road a former Victorian school has gained recent additions – not uncomplimentary – now serving as a Hindu temple. Lozells was a small village between Aston Manor and Handsworth and became part of the city of Birmingham in the 1830s when it was still a borough.

Local architect J. A. Chatwin had a hand in several ecclesiastical buildings, notably St Paul's (1880) where he used Bath stone on the west front. The terraced houses were laid out well and the work of the Birmingham Freehold Land Society to end back to backs bore fruit in the 1850s.

Heathfield Road is the main thoroughfare between Aston and Soho Hill. Oddly Villa Road is at the Handsworth end, while across the A34 Walsall Road, it is Trinity Road leading to Villa Park, Aston. North along the A34 is the suburb of Birchfields leading to Perry Barr. Here is the River Tame, flowing east, having made its way from Bescot (near the present Walsall Town stadium) where the three head streams join together.

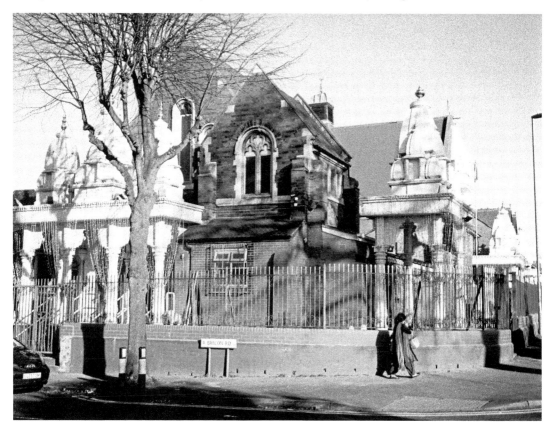

New life of old Victorian school.

River Tame, Perry Bridges

The A34, a key trunk road from Southampton Docks to Preston Docks, was one of the first to be 'dualled'. At Perry Bridges it crossed the River Tame. Here the old stone packhorse bridge has been retained as a footbridge by the art deco stressed-concrete bridge of the 1930s.

Traffic on the Walsall Road cannot appreciate the architecture or history at road level. Downstream the Tame Valley was industrialised from the mid-1800s, flowing through Witton, Nechells, Washwood Heath, Bromford to Castle Vale and Fort Dunlop – Not that you would know the largest tributary of England's biggest river flows this way as it is hidden by competing canals, railway, motorway and factories.

Ironically a riverside path exists between Aston and Gravelley Hill, but the grassy banks of the Tame from Sandwell Park to Perry Barr aren't, but there's no motorway above!

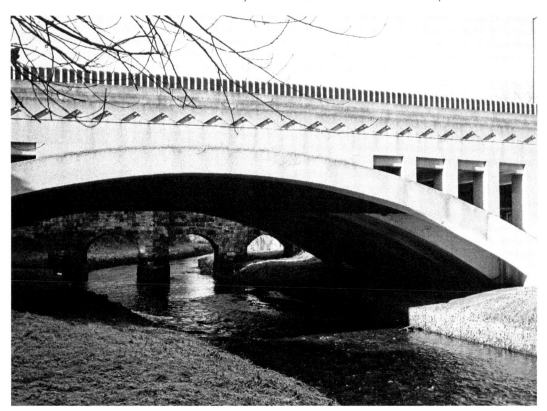

Art deco at work: A34 bridge over the River Tame.

Kingstanding

Kingstanding is the highest land in the north of the city at 548 feet above sea level. Which king stood here and why? Submerged by a 1930s housing development built by Birmingham, it was equal to the size of Shrewsbury when populated between the wars. It was previously part of Great Barr, then Perry Barr Urban District until 1931, when Staffordshire gave it up as its ultimate sacrifice from the hundred of Offlow. Dr Robert Plot, cartographer, has indicated Kingstanding on his map of Staffordshire dated 1686. Charles I passed this way before descending to Camphill. It was thought to be a royal viewpoint between the forests of Arden and Needwood or where the king oversaw his army of troops. Recent archaeology has indicated a prehistoric burial mound dating back to 2500 BC – making this site the oldest man-made structure in the city. The nearest known hill fort is Castle Ring, north of here on Cannock Chase.

Unlike the Roman fort at Metchley/Queen Elizabeth Medical Centre, it hasn't been built all over! Regrettably much intensive ploughing has removed a great deal of earthwork structure.

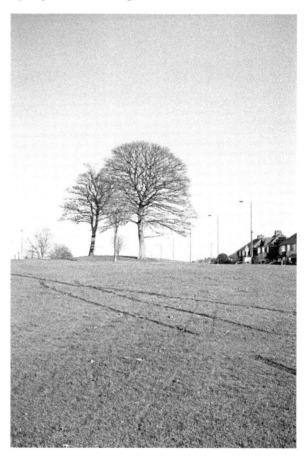

At nearly 600 feet, this was once a burial tumulus.

Newman University College, Bartley Green

The story of Newman College begins on the opposite side of the city. It was named after Cardinal John Newman, who established a Catholic seminary at Oscott on the Chester Road – becoming Oscott College. Its role of training novice priests ceased when the college was founded.

In 1968 Newman College was founded as a teacher training college on a new site in West Birmingham at Bartley Green, named after Cardinal Newman, who himself had taught at Cotton College for boys in North Staffordshire. He was interred at Rednall in the shadow of the Lickey Hills. With the decision to beatify Newman, his remains have been removed to the Vatican.

An astrolabe in shinny steel has appeared at the revamped entrance of Newman College on Cromwell Lane, Bartley Green.

DID YOU KNOW?

John Newman (1801–90) had been an Anglican priest before converting to Catholicism. He officiated at the opening of St Wilfred's Church (Cotton, north Staffordshire) recently completed by A. W. N. Pugin in 1848 for the Earl of Shrewsbury. As an Oratorian church it was not in a suitable location, plus the fact Newman considered the 'gothick' unsuitable for an oratory – within a year he had established the Birmingham oratory at Oscott in 1849.

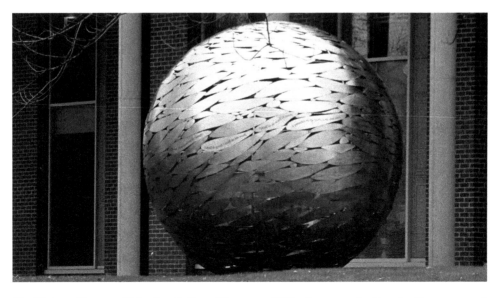

The Globe at Newman Univeristy College. (Courtesy of Elliot Brown under Creative Commons 2.0)

St Peter's Parish Church, Harborne

Standing at 564 feet above sea level is Harborne's ancient parish church – St Peter's. Its large red sandstone tower dates back to the fifteenth century. The rest of the fabric has been replaced. The village near the church retains much of a rural atmosphere. Harborne celebrated Queen Victoria's Golden Jubilee with the opening of Queens Park along Court Oak Road – it was free to the public. Court Oak is the main road junction and alludes to ancient manorial court systems. The lord of the manor dispensed fines and penalties for feudal infringements. Lord Calthorpe was the chief landowner in Harborne and Edgbaston. Local residents voted to join Birmingham, tempted by lower rates, in 1891.

DID YOU KNOW?

Harborne appears as 'Horborne' in the Domesday Book of 1086, with land being held by the Bishop of Chester for a plough, unlike nearby Handsworth, which had two ploughs – six villages with four smallholders with two ploughs, and one of sixty-six places in the Offlow hundred of Staffordshire. A mill was recorded and 2 acres of meadows and woodland at a value of 20 shillings. The land was held by Williamson of Ansculf. His main land holding was in West Bromwich.

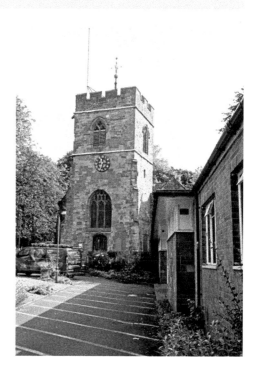

The fine sandstone tower of Harborne, Staffordshire.

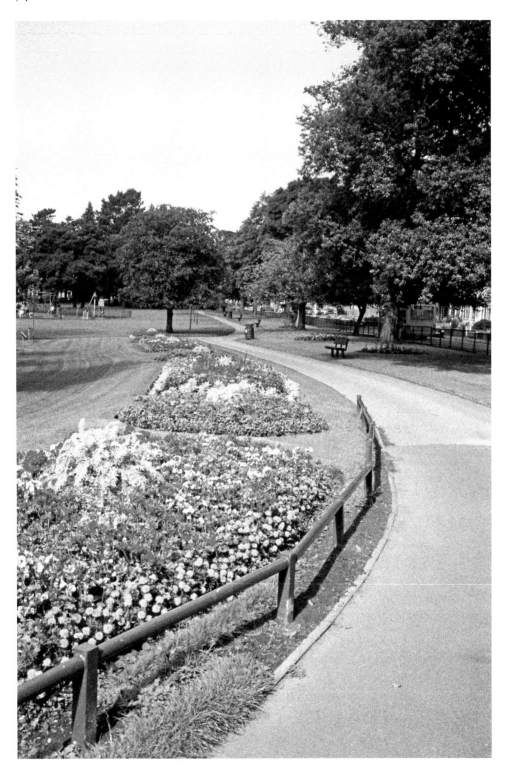

One of Birmingham's thirty-two parks: Queens Park, Harborne.

Queens Park, Court Oak Road, Harborne

Birmingham has over thirty-two parks, with over 32,000 acres of public open space in 260 areas and a dozen lakes and nature reserves. The largest is Sutton Park, which has Exmoor ponies grazing in it. Queens Park is a splendid spot in the middle of the village and has a fascinating row of villas along its western side. The Calthorpes of Edgbaston controlled their Harborne portfolio, commissioning John Harris with the layout of the whole estate. Nearby Moorpool estate was an attempt to replicate a garden village such as Cadbury's Bournville.

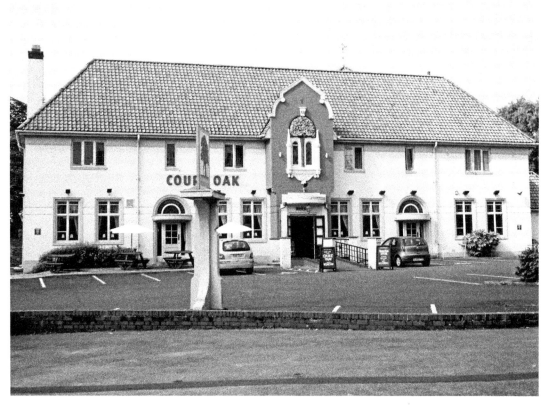

Court Oak.

Five Ways, Islington

Five Ways was in existence since before 1565, when it was officially recorded. The clock is a memorial to the anti-slave campaigner Joseph Sturge. Behind this is Metropolitan House, built in 1964, apparently designed by Seymour Harris. Broad Street leads to the city centre, while Islington Row is now part of the middle ring road. Calthorpe Road leads to Edgbaston, Harborne Road to Harborne and Hagley Road to Quiton and Halesowen. The tower was built a year before the Rotunda but that has Grade I-listed status and is taller at 265 feet, compared with 223 feet – both have recently been refurbished.

The epitaph of Joseph Sturge reads, 'He lived to bring freedom to the negro slave, the vote to the British working man and the promise of peace to a war torn world.'

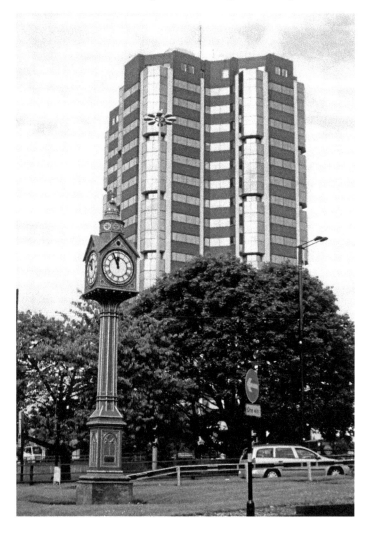

Five Ways clock tower erected in remembrance of anti-slave campaigner Joseph Sturge.

Digbeth High Street

Looking up to the Bull Ring, a range of architectural styles from Victorian Gothic to 1960s Rotunda and space age Selfridges 'blobbyscape' can be seen. St Martins in the Bull Ring looks rather glum – its red sandstone sparkles in the sunshine! The tombs of DeBermynghems are within. The spire is 200 feet tall. The Bull Ring gets its name from the ring of iron to which livestock were tied ready for sale. How many times has the odd getaway galloped down Digbeth High Street to wander off into Deritend? Now it's dammed up with the flow of vehicles storming along the dual carriageway on the A34 (Stratford Road).

The River Rea flows under the road – the old boundary between Digbeth and Deritend and the tow respective High Streets. Balsall Heath was incorporated into the newly created city along with Edgbaston, Harborne, Saltley District Council and Little Bromwich Urban District Council in 1891.

DID YOU KNOW?

Birmingham's Queensway ring road was trialled for 'Grand Prix' racing in the 1980s.

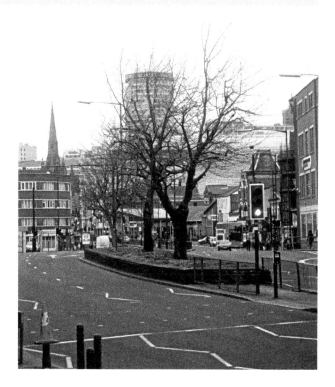

Looking from the Old Crown to the Rotunda. Does the River Rea cross here somewhere?

River Bourne, Selly Oak

The River Bourne begins under Egg Hill near Frankley and flows into the River Rea at Stirtchley; not to be confused with Bournebrook further north, which also flows onto the Rea but at Cannon Hill Park near Pebble Mill.

The Cadbury brothers chose this location for their cocoa and chocolate factory in 1879. George and Richard were Quakers and took their responsibility in looking after their workforce seriously. They built Bourneville village in 1895–1900 to house the increasing number of employees. By 1900 there were 6,000 people. Good communications attracted the Cadburys to this location, adjacent to the Birmingham & Worcester Canal with links to Gloucester Docks, completed in 1815. The West Birmingham Railway was built in 1876, initially as single track, but improved and by 1904 there were direct rail links to their factory.

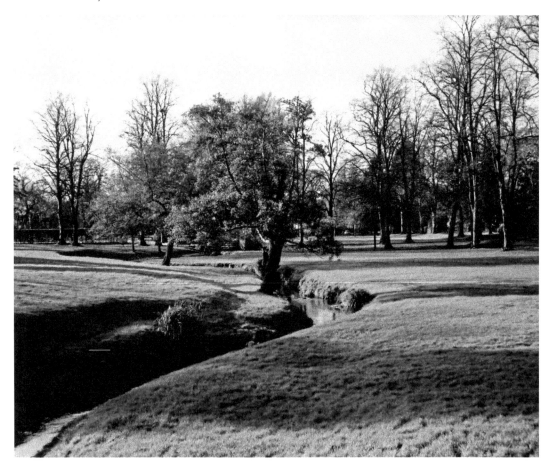

Part of Cadbury's dream.

Cadbury Schools and Memorial Carillon, Bournville

George Cadbury saw education as being key to a fulfilled life for his families. He was ahead of his time and, when offering the Bournville school to the local authority, they were concerned that his classrooms could only take forty-five pupils. They baulked at the expense of employing an extra teacher. Cadbury added the Carillon Tower after visiting Bruges. He installed twenty-two bells, cast by the famous Loughborough bell foundry. Later bells were added after George's death in 1922, so today there are forty-eight bells. Eventually the schools were taken over by Birmingham City Council, who adopted their standards.

Nearby Ruskin Hall was built as a village institute and college for adult education. It is now part of the School of Art of University of Central England for aspiring jewellers and silversmiths. The Bournville estate was a total of 612 acres and includes two rescued historic buildings – Selly Oak Manor and Minworth Greaves.

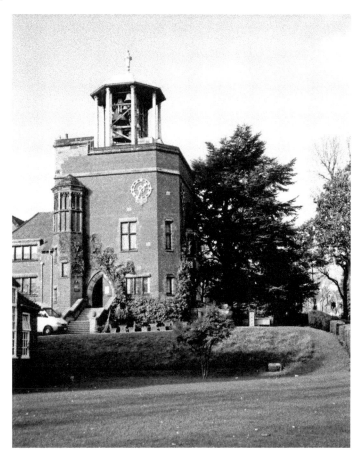

Cadbury Schools and Memorial Carillon, Bournville.

Rest House and Ruskin Hall, Bournville Green

Viewed from the small parade of shops on Sycamore Road, above the factory, is the village green rest house. Modelled on the Yarn market at Dunster, it celebrates the silver wedding of George and Elizabeth Cadbury and was built in 1914. A total of 16 acres were set aside for 'green' spaces, parks and playgrounds.

At the top of the green is Ruskin Hall, opposite the Friends Meeting House (off right). William A. Harvey was Cadbury's architect for all estate buildings and the overall scheme layout. The Rest House is also a lasting memorial to George Cadbury. His ashes are contained under the bust inside the house. On 28 October 1922 over 16,000 people attended the memorial service on the green, to the accompaniment of his favourite tunes of hymns on the carillon.

DID YOU KNOW?

Both the Cadbury and Fry families were Quakers and were close – both making chocolate, the Frys in Bristol. Eventually the companies merged with factories at Leominster, Knighton (Staffs) and Keynsham, becoming part of Cadburys by the twentieth century. Upon George Cadbury's death in Bournville on 24 October 1922, he was cremated at Perry Barr. Sixteen thousand people gathered on the green for his memorial service.

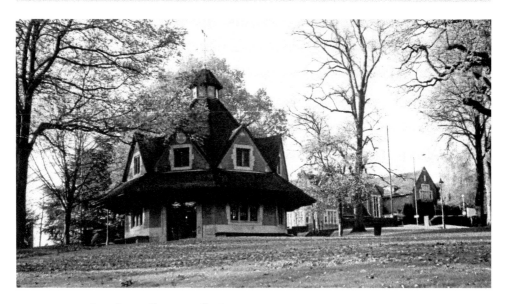

Rest House and Ruskin Hall, Bournville Green.

Dale End Square/Clock Court, formerly Dalton Street

The east side of the centre of the city has been greatly altered. Gone are the YMCA and St Bartholomew's Church, demolished in 1943. Dalton Walk records the former Dalton Street, which ran parallel to Corporation Street (seen in the background). The square clock tower has been restored. Priory Walk, which links the square to Old Square, is the only reminder of St Thomas's Priory – an Augustinian foundation that survived until 1547 when it was dissolved by Wolseley.

Wolseley Carriage Co., Saltley, was the first car manufacturers in Britain – a very young Herbert Austin, who later established the Longbridge Works, was an early driver for Wolseley.

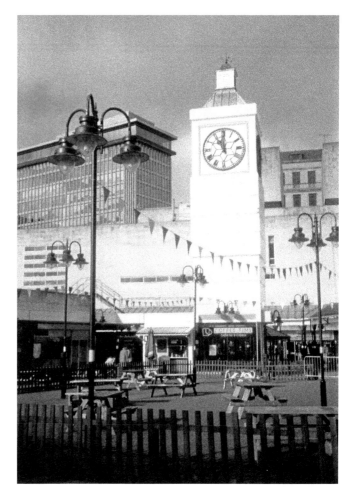

Dalton Walk clock tower.

Fire Headquarters/Central Fire Station, Lancaster Circus

Built as the city of Birmingham Fire Brigade Headquarters in 1934 on Mosshouse Lane, it is in fact a triangular building with an inner courtyard. The tower is above the main entrance. Along the Corporation Street side are the eleven-bay 'red' doors for the dispatch of the fire pumps.

Lancaster Circus was built later in the early 1960s. Behind the West Midlands Fire HQ is the Costa Green, main building of Aston University, which dates from 1951. The site was acquired in 1933 but was delayed due to the Second World War. Originally founded in 1875 as the School of Metallurgy, it has over 9,500 students with a greatly expanded campus. Research includes photonics, neuroimaging, energy and vision sciences. Recent success has been the development of Tamozolomide to tackle brain cancer.

A new Fire and Rescue HQ has been built and this buildings future is uncertain – maybe Aston University could put it to use?

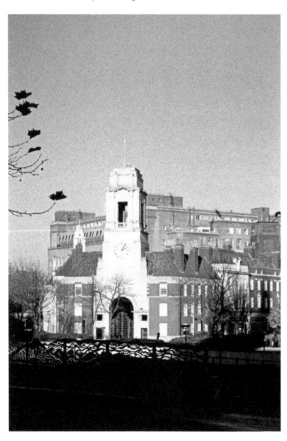

Lancaster Circus Central Fire Station.

Central Methodist Hall, Steelhouse

Reflecting the design of the Victorian Law Courts, opposite is the Methodist Central Hall. It was built in 1903/4 in the middle of Corporation Street (Old Square to Lancaster Circus). The new Crown Courts are behind Central Hall, off James Watt Street. The building was listed as Grade II in 1970 and now forms the core of the Steelhouse conservation area. Internally it still retains the original grand staircase and organ.

The impressive 200-foot tower predates the Chamberlain Tower of Birmingham University. The architects of Central Hall were J. and E. Harper, while Aston Webb was responsible for the Victorian law courts on the opposite side of Corporation Street.

Nonconformism was an important driving force in Birmingham, as with England's other great industrial cities such as Manchester. Many of the city's influential wealthy families were members of non-Anglican churches.

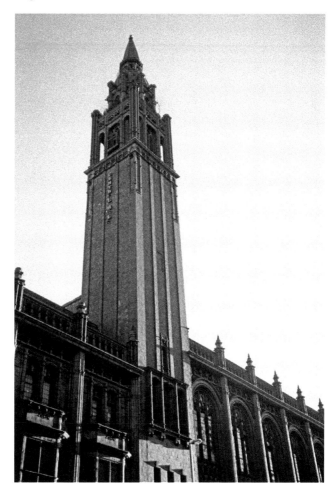

Central Methodist Hall, Steelhouse.

Wesleyan General Building, Snow Hill/ Colmore Circus

The bottom end of Colmore Row/Snow Hill has been extensively redevelopment. The Wesleyan General Insurance building is one of Birmingham's oldest Friendly Societies. The main bank branches are to be found along Colmore Row, which forms the north side of Cathedral Square. Ever taller buildings are hemming in the neoclassical church.

The Great Western Arcade alludes to the Great Western Railway, who built the original station at Snow Hill in 1852.

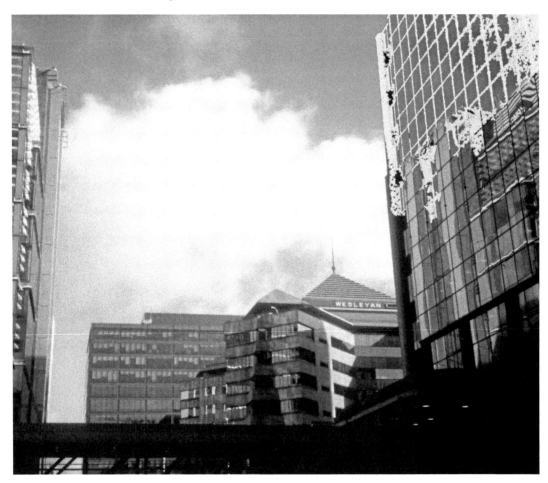

Wesleyan General Building, Snow Hill/Colmore Circus.

Jewellery Quarter

Birmingham's jewellery district is the largest concentration of specialist metalworkers in Europe. Pen nibs, buttons, medals and fine jewellery can all be found in the Summertown/Newtown area. Britain's largest Assay Office is also located here, having recently moved from Newhall Street to Pope Street. Mathew Boulton campaigned to have Birmingham get its Assay Office back in 1773, as hitherto the nearest were Chester and London.

From manufacturing of pen nibs, Chamberlain and Nettlefield became one of Europe's largest engineering firms – GKN. The Chamberlains became Birmingham's leading political family between 1869 and 1939. On Frederick Street is the Pen Museum, close by is the unusual and surprising Coffin Works museum of Newman Brothers (on Fleet Street, off Newhall Street); 'it's not what you might expect'. At the northern end of the Jewellery Quarter, on Vyse Street – the top end of Frederick Street – is the Museum of the Jewellery Quarter, found in the former workshops of Smith & Pepper.

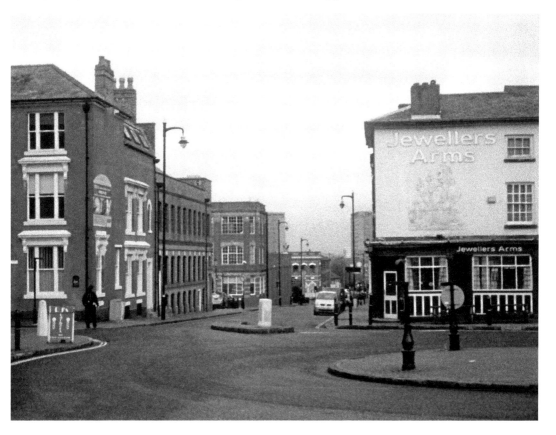

Heart of the revitalised Jewellery Quarter (Jewellers Arms).

Duchy of Cornwall Estate Gate

A fine example of the iron-makers craft can be seen in the courtyard gates of the JCB part of the Duchy of Cornwall estates. Kings Norton to the south was a royal manor until 1804, when George II sold it. The manor was granted to Hugo Bardin in 1200 along with the manor of Bromsgrove. Edward IV granted the manors to the Duchess of York, in whose possession they remained until George II sold it off.

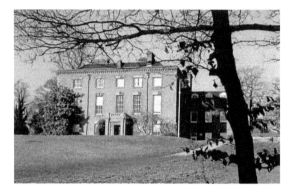

Edgbaston Hall.

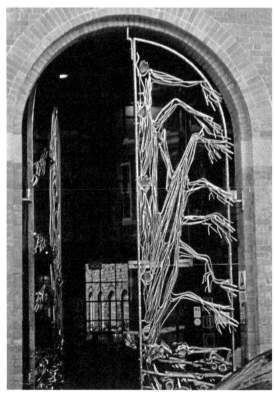

Duchy of Cornwall Estate gate, Jewellery Quarter.

Old St Bartholomew's, Edgbaston

On the hill above the tributary valley of Chad Brook in the River Rea is the square towered red sandstone church adjacent to Edgbaston Hall. The hall was once the home of botanist William Withering, discoverer of 'digitalis'. Now the clubhouse of Edgbaston Golf Club, it makes a pleasant vale with two lakes separating the old village centre from the ever-expanding academic village of Birmingham University.

Chad Valley is perhaps better known by children of the 1950s and '60s for its die-cast metal models and games production in Harborne.

Arthur Mee's *Warwickshire* says, 'The church is full of beautiful things'. William Withering founded Birmingham's first hospital. Humphrey Middlemore was a staunch Catholic and was martyred. The Gough and Calthorpe families are interred within the ancient fabric.

Back in the 1930s he described the landscape as 'forest scenery of the grandest kind, less than 2 miles from the city centre'. Calthorpe fields lie between Edgbaston and the city centre but are an open space no more. Calthorpe Park, through which the Elan Aqueduct flows in its subterranean pipes, is adjacent to the River Rea, a mile south-east of Edgbaston church.

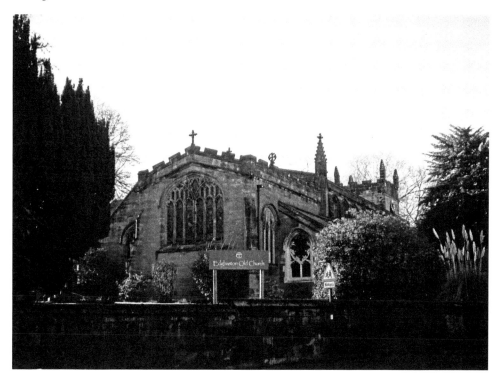

Edgbaston Old Church.

St Mary's, Moseley

Mosely was once a small village due south of the city centre, on the Alcester Road, and occupying high ground between the Rea and Cole valleys. At the crossroads of the B4217 Edgbaston to Hall Green is the square towered parish church. Dating back to the sixteenth century, the dulled red-sandstone church watches the junction below – it still retains a village atmosphere and a post office.

Up the hill is the famous Moseley School, built in 1857, designed by Joseph James. As with other large buildings, such as Highbury, it was sequestered during the First World War as an injury recovery centre. Today it is a comprehensive school.

Highbury was built for Joseph Chamberlain, industrialist, local politician and statesman, and was given to the city by Austin Chamberlain. Highbury Park is open to the public. To the north is Cannon Hill Park and due south is Kings Heath Park, separated by the railway.

St Mary's Church was referred to in 1405 as within the Kings Norton parish under the auspices of Bromsgrove Priory. It had to wait until 1866 to become a full parish. It's 'Robed Choir' is nationally known, regularly performing in Anglican cathedrals and churches.

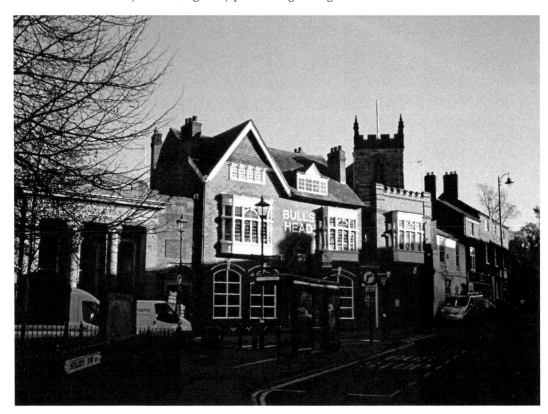

The Bull's Head in Moseley High Street.

Moseley Hall

It was designed by an unrelated J. H. Chamberlain, with many of the fittings made by Pugin's manufacturer J. Hardman. It was probably the first house in Birmingham to be gas lit in 1880. When Joseph Chamberlain was mayor, he made great reforms to improve the city centre – with water and gas supply, housing, education and criminal justice.

As a Liberal Unionist he held office as Secretary to the Colonies, and Chancellor of Trade. As a nonconformist Unitarian, he declined self-aggrandisement of titles. Under the 1878 Improvement Scheme, Corporation Street was planned, giving the city centre a good 'High Street' and ridding it of the slums of the rookery.

New law courts were built halfway down the new Corporation Street; these have now been superseded with new Crown Courts off Watt Place, and the County/Magistrates' Court now occupy the old buildings.

Chamberlain's great legacy to Birmingham is the University at Edgbaston. He was a governor of its predecessor, Mason College, in 1875. He raised £1 million for the university to begin its construction but sadly suffered a stroke and was unable to attend the official opening by the king, on 7 July 1909.

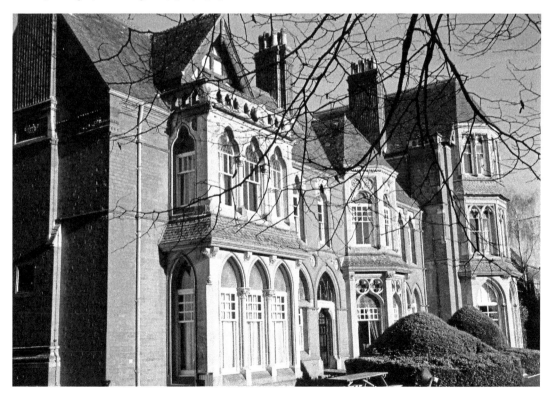

Highbury, Moseley.

Symphony Hall

Dominated by the thirty-car, 1,801-foot-high Ferris wheel at the western end of the plaza, adjacent to the International Convention Centre, is Birmingham's Symphony Hall – one of the best acoustically in the world – and the Repertory Theatre. It has since been joined halfway along by the 'birds nest' Library of Birmingham. Why we need to build a new one every forty years is unknown. The inverted zigzag of 1974 by John Madin had eventually been accepted by and large. This one will be Birmingham's fourth Central Library. One of its notable collections is its Shakespeare Memorial Library – the largest in the world.

At the eastern end, opposite the 1930s neoclassical Baskerville House, is Birmingham's Hall of Memory/Remembrance. It is open every day for the turning of the page of the Book of Remembrance.

The square was dedicated in 1989, celebrating the 100th anniversary of the city of Birmingham. It was planned in the 1920s to be a grand civic square, but only the eastern end was built before the Great Depression, and the Second World War interrupted its completion. It's a pity that all that remains of the £3 million spent on 'public art' here in the early 1990s is only the 'lumpy, bumpy, cracked brick paving'.

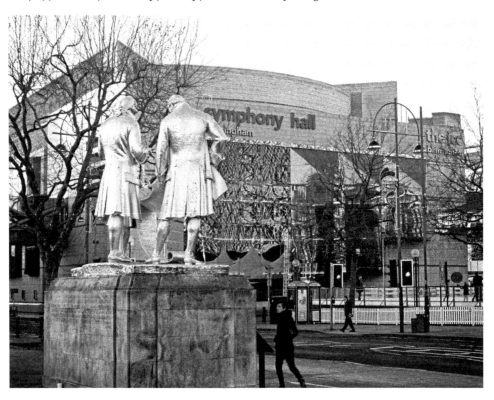

Symphony Hall stands on the site of Birmingham's first Exhibition Hall off Broad Street.

Library of Birmingham

Many collections can be found in the Library of Birmingham, not least the 30,000 books in over fifty languages of the Shakespeare Library, always being added to regarding Warwickshire's most famous son.

Here, too, are the finest collections of William Morris books printed by the Kelmscott Press, who collaborated with Burne-Jones and others creating the Arts and Crafts style. Several of his works belong to the city and are exhibited in the art gallery in Chamberlain Square.

Also in the library are the collections of James Watt and Mathew Boulton. His statue stood alongside Birmingham's original library. Over 30,000 of Benjamin Stones' photographs are kept here along with poems of John Drinkwater and works of both natives and visitors alike that have links to the city can be found inside. Like its predecessor, it attracts visitors from far and wide, so much so that Sunday opening was necessary when it opened in 2013. Pity Chamberlain Square is a mess while they redevelop the old brutalist site.

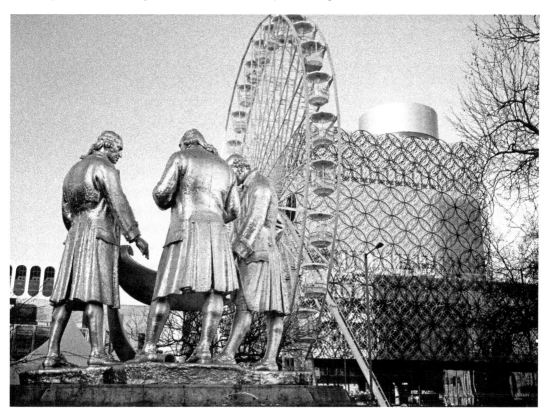

Birmingham's fourth library. Let's hope this one lasts as long as the previous one, now in Centenary Square.

Boulton, Murdoch and Watt, Broad Street

Erected in 1956, the bronze gilt statue representing the 'three musketeers' studying a chart was made by William Bloye (1890–1975), and has recently been regilded. It has survived much longer than the recent Raymond Mason 'forward' sculpture, which stood opposite in Centenary Plaza, which as a highly inflammable fiberglass/resin/paint construct was melted out of recognition (by a stray cigarette possibly?) and had to be dismantled.

Matthew Boulton (1728–1809), the inventor and manufacturer, brought James Watt (1736–1819), the developer of the steam engine, with William Murdoch (1754–1839), who found out how to make coal gas and developed its use.

In Gas Street is the oldest surviving gas retort house in the world, dating from 1822. The famous Canal Basin is more widely known.

Centenary Square was created by the reclamation of the Gibson's canal basin and demolition of the Bingley exhibition hall, which had suffered a major fire in1984. New Bingley Hall was built at the Staffordshire Show Ground, Stafford and the land sold to the City Council.

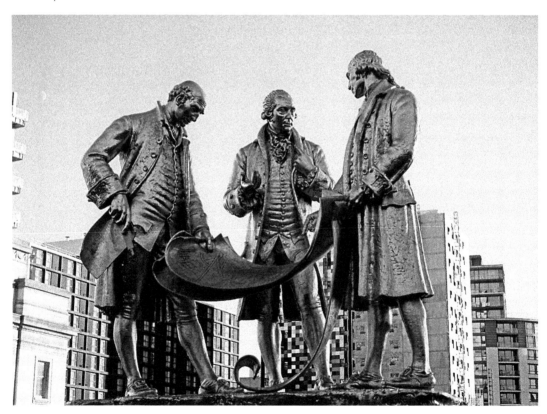

The statue to BMW – the founders of modern Birmingham.

Brindley Place

At the heart of Brindley Place today is the Ikon Gallery, greatly overshadowed by glass and concrete. Its unusual architecture for 1877 was one of Birmingham's board schools following the 1870 Education Act. It is a three-storey, warm red-brick building with small turret tower and seven bays, with a square bell/clock tower, taller than the round tower.

A pioneering art gallery since the 1990s, it is now an internationally acclaimed contemporary gallery showing works from around the world. Visitors can enjoy free exhibitions, talks, workshops and tours.

The only other pre-1990s building hereabouts is the second oldest Church of Christ the Scientist, which faces the Hyatt Hotel. In 1769 James Brindley can claim to have brought power to Birmingham – coal from Wednesbury – and provided the means for raw materials too. Once one waterway had been built, the success of moving 'finished goods' relied on the expansion of the 'grand cross' of England's canals, all focused on Birmingham. This scheme was primarily supported by Lunar Society member Josiah Wedgwood of North Staffordshire. He cuts the first sod of the Trent & Mersey Canal at Burslem in 1766.

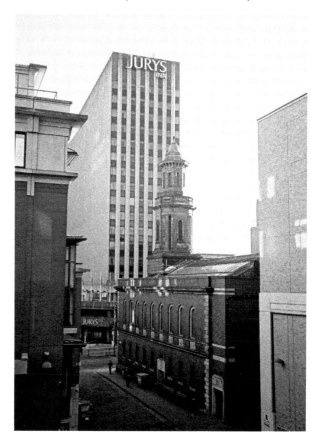

One of only two buildings more than 100 years old left in this part of the city.

Warstone Necropolis, Hockley

As Birmingham grew, so did its deceased population, and the wealthy Victorians laid their cemeteries out as they did their parks. Opened in 1847 to a design by J. R. Hamilton, it has a two-tier horseshoe-shaped catacomb.

During the Second World War local people resorted to sheltering during bombing raids inside the catacombs. Today it is a Grade II-listed site on the register of Historic Parks and Gardens. It contains many interesting monuments and is open to the public.

It was in west Birmingham that after the charter of 1842 the 'sorry trio of institutions were established', namely the Borough Goal, Asylum and Workhouse, all at Winson Green.

DID YOU KNOW?

There are traces of twelve greens in the names of suburbs within the city – from Brown's Green and Acock's Green in the north-east to Hall Green and Bartley Green in the south-west. They are more widely known as Winson Green, Bordesley Green and Wylde Green.

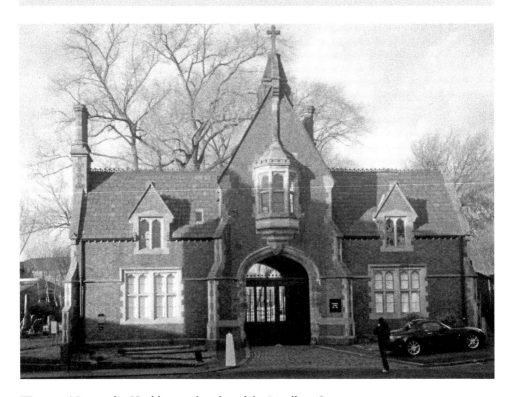

Warstone Necropolis, Hockley, on the edge of the Jewellery Quarter.

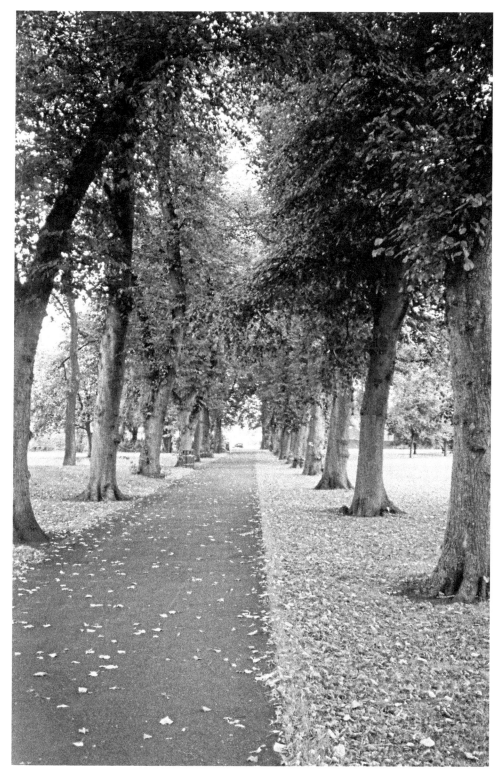

An area more commonly known as Winson Green, Boredesley Green and Wylde Green.

Calthorpe Park and Balsall Heath

Named after Lord Calthorpe of Edgbaston, who would think that millions of gallons of Welsh water flows beneath this path on its way to St Martins Market and Aston Reservoir. Much of this part of the city has been rebuilt since the Second World War. The River Rea also flows through the park. The view from the top of Balsall Heath Road 'across a bit of a heath' extends to the city centre skyline.

One of the ten 'Heaths' give their name to parts of the city – Balsall Heath is a temporary remnant close to the city centre. Near the middle ring road, it won't have this view for long, as development is nigh due. The skyline of the city centre shows the diversity of Birmingham in more ways than one, but what would one expect of 'the city of a thousand trades'?

The Lapal Canal headed west off the Birmingham & Worcester Canal and provided the only direct link via the Lapal Tunnel across the Sedgeley-Northfield ridge to Stourbridge and the River Severn there.

The City of Birmingham College has a campus at Millennium Point. This side of the city has been traditionally dominated by Aston University of Technology. Many Victorian suburbs were bulldozed to create it in the 1960s. Indeed Aston, home of the 'Villa', was a separate borough.

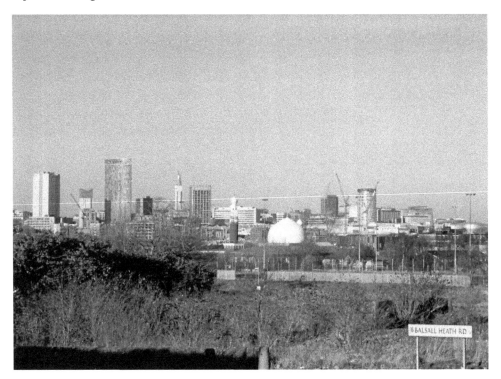

The remnant of one of eight 'heaths' to be found within the city boundary.